THE PEACHY EXPERIENCE

A 40-Day Prayer Journal for Living Life Authentically

By

Sarah L. Henley

The Peachy Experience

A 40-day prayer journal for living life authentically

Book design by Sarah L. HENLEY

Published AND PRINTED by kindle direct publishing
Kdp.amazon.com

FOREWORD

Ten years ago, I was a "super senior" in college at T (North Carolina Agricultural & Technical State University), working a full-time job, serving in a church ministry at church every Sunday, and *still* not completely sure of who I was. My solid foundation and belief that Jesus is Lord always sobered me up and kept me from drowning in my shortcomings. However, the trauma of my childhood and the shame caused by some of my early adulthood decisions served as a barrier between the Sarah that God knew and the Sarah that everyone else got to see.

I loved saying that everything was "Peachy," but in the depths of my soul, I was far from it. I longed to close the gap and be myself, but I experienced rejection in the very places *and* from the very people I depended on for affirmation. And so, I was perplexed with how to be myself *and* stay in right standing with God. By the grace of God, I decided to start fresh after years of running from myself and God. I rededicated my life to Christ and began practicing the discipline of fasting right away. It was in those periods of denying myself the comforts and enjoyments that I'd normally use to self-medicate, where I learned to hear the voice of God and embark on the journey of becoming authentically me.

As I continually presented myself before God, all of my trauma and illegitimate identity exposed, I experienced His divine intervention and finally began to heal. The journey to becoming whole and *staying* whole has been hard work. It has only been perfected through prayer, meditation in the word of God, therapy, consistently enforcing healthy boundaries, and being a committed and constant learner.

For nearly four years, I've labored off and on between states (Maryland, North Carolina, and Arizona), getting married, giving birth, and serious illness, to bring forth this intimate journey which God has released me to share. Here lies only 40 of the 480 journal entries I composed to myself and prayers that I prayed to God which have been documented on a paper hanger (lol) and in my phone since 2008. I am honored to publish some of the personal revelations that I believe have served as the blueprint for establishing and maintaining strong faith throughout my evolution into who I am today. This is my assignment, and my courage to fulfil it was inspired by the desire to encourage other sisters, daughters, and mothers.

Through this sobering labor of love, I especially hope to inspire those springing up out of troubled beginnings and those who long to reconcile a childhood foundation of faith in Christ that at any time was left unnurtured. It is also my fervent prayer that all who read this journal will accept the gift of Jesus Christ.

John 3:16 "For God so loved the world that he gave his only Son, that whoever believes in him shall not perish but have eternal life."

Dedicated to my husband, Tom, and children, Thomas, Jr., Violet, & Hazel, with love.

DAY 1

1 John 4:1-6 NIV "1 Dear friends, do not believe every spirit, but test the spirits to see whether they are from God, because many false prophets have gone out into the world. 2 This is how you can recognize the Spirit of God: Every spirit that acknowledges that Jesus Christ has come in the flesh is from God, 3 but every spirit that does not acknowledge Jesus is not from God. This is the spirit of the antichrist, which you have heard is coming and even now is already in the world. 4 You, dear children, are from God and have overcome them, because the one who is in you is greater than the one who is in the world. 5 They are from the world and therefore, speak from viewpoint of the world, and the world listens to them. 6 We are from God, and whoever knows God listens to us; but whoever is not from God does not listen to us. This is how we recognize the Spirit of truth and the spirit of falsehood."

IF YOU MUST SLAY...

If you must slay anything, slay generational curses! I'm talking 2 Samuel 23:20-21, Benaiah (son of Jehoiada) slay. Lol. You have to be willing to walk away from untruths no matter who the source of the untruth is. I've found this most difficult within the family unit. The difficulty could be because one of my spiritual gifts is mercy, or it could just be that "obedience to God's will and instruction by any means necessary" attitude kicking in. Either way, stepping out of your comfort zone is very difficult to do, especially when people you love are in it.

It is human nature to seek advice and the opinions of others, but once we accept Jesus, it is our responsibility to do what pleases God first and foremost. You are destined to live a life full of prosperity, but you can't live right based off of the wrong information. Repeating the same mistakes as those who came before you is simply unnecessary. I believe this is why God gives each of us different point of views, even when faced with the same situations. He made each of us unique.

Absence of identity and imitating what others do can *rob* us of our God given uniqueness. This is not to say that we shouldn't heed wisdom. However, imitation can be a doorway to idolatry, which is never okay. Admiration is good, but always be in prayer for God to give clear and specific instructions. Many times, what we have been groomed to adopt is not actually what we should practice.

Generational shortcomings are often the result of a single, yet, subtle untruth that made someone in our lineage feel good. And unfortunately, as we all know: the tale gets juicier from person to person. Each time the story is told, something is added and what was once said or done incorrectly with good intentions becomes further and further from the truth. The instant gratification of one person can unintentionally pollute, and what people tell you to do often differs from what they would do if presented with the same set of circumstances themselves. That isn't a crime. It is, however, a reason for you to go to GOD first. The word says in 1 Peter 5:7 NIV "Cast all your anxiety on him because he cares for you." Pray, and ask God for the discernment you need. Don't let generational curses dictate your path. Slay those generational curses and leave them where they lie. Do it now! Don't worry about who disagrees. Your approval comes from God. Work what Our Father in heaven gave us– The Word!!!

Lord,

Today I come to you, praying against the very falsehoods that have preyed on me and generations of family that came before me. It often seems so hard to stand, when people I love aren't standing with me, but I know that you have not forgotten me. Please grant me the patience to war in the spiritual realm for my family to come to know your truths and your will for our lives Please forgive me for ignoring your truth at times, in moments when my fear and dependence on what may have felt right lured me outside of your will.

Thank you for your grace and mercy. Thank you for your strength, for use in times of struggle and strife in my family dynamic. Please help us to not be lost in our own agendas forever, but rather, help us come to know what your word says about who we are and what we are yet to become in Christ. I curse every curse sewn into my family and I arrest every demonic belief and rumor that has previously permeated the spirits of every single person in my family, from generation to generation. I ask that you block every imp and demonic principality that has subtly communed with us. Please don't let another curse be carried into our future.

In Jesus' Name, Amen

DAY 2

Psalms 128:1 NIV "Blessed are all who fear the Lord, who walk in obedience to him."

OBEDIENCE BY UNPOPULAR DEMAND

There is truth to the statement that there is more than one way to skin a cat, but don't let that belief be the death of you. Better than figuring out how to get each skinning technique down to a science, be concerned with the way YOU are supposed to do it. Even more than that, be concerned with the way you are supposed to do it in *this* season of your life. It is so easy to miss the mark and misinterpret the message of metaphors due to familiarity. Using the same approach in a different situation can cause unnecessary damage spiritually, physically, emotionally, and even financially.

Likewise, it is also unwise to favor skill over strategy. In order to receive strategy, you have to know where it comes from. The source of good strategy is God. Your next test may provoke you to rely on your strengths or that of your inner circle, but I encourage you set a new standard for yourself and strive to do what *God* is nudging you to do. It may be your norm to do what you think is best, but is that what God is telling you to do? Has *He* affirmed this course of action?

If you consider yourself among those who abide in Him, an unwavering conviction will always arise inside of you when what you plan to do is outside of the Will of God. In John 15:4 NIV, Jesus Christ advises us "Abide in me, and I in you. As the branch cannot bear fruit of itself, except it abide in the vine; no more can ye, except ye abide in me."

In this life, being deceived will be easy, doing what is best for you will feel good, and pleasing people will be the cross many choose to bear. My advice: prioritize obedience to God. The rest will follow.

Lord,

I want to please you but I admit don't know how to do that on my own. I need you to point me in the right direction. My ask in this season is that you block anxiety and grant me your peace. Help me to crave the truth and give me your discernment so that I will do what pleases you, even when others and my own understanding make me feel bad for it. I am grateful that you are committed to caring for my every need, and I trust that you have all the answers to every question I will ever ask. Cause my desires to align with your will. Empower me to exercise full discernment and obedience. For your glory, forever.

In Jesus' Name, Amen.

DAY 3

2 Timothy 3:14-15 NIV "14 But as for you, continue in what you have learned and have become convinced of, because you know those from whom you learned it, 15 and how from infancy you have known the Holy Scriptures, which are able to make you wise for salvation through faith in Christ Jesus."

DON'T GET CAUGHT UP IN THE "WHY"

I know it's hard to walk away from it without knowing why, but my dear, the reality is: the "why" doesn't really matter. There are things we will never know and I believe that there is a reason for that. The Bible says in James 1:5 NIV, "If any of you lacks wisdom, you should ask God, who gives generously to all without finding fault, and it will be given to you."

We have to accept God's generous wisdom as WHOLE, instead of finding HOLES in it when His answer does not fit the parameters of our reasoning and logic. This can be specifically hard to do when we have been wronged or slighted. Equally difficult, is finding the restraint to avoid attempting to reason within ourselves about why we have wronged or slighted others. Self-reflection is good, but getting hung up on "why" is a trap. In my experience, getting an explanation lacks importance compared to simple acceptance of what it is or isn't at face value.

Some of us will beat the wheels off of our wagon, trying to get to the bottom of something, only to discover the reason "why" and deem it inadequate in relation to our expectations. It is so much easier to simply adopt a posture of gratitude for what happened because you *survived* what happened. That is the miracle. We waste energy and precious time, unless it is our occupation, when we pursue avenue after avenue of what we think is going to lead us to the reason behind something. Half of the time we have already discerned the entity at play, but when we aren't satisfied with what the Holy Spirit has said, we keep digging.

It is completely fine to want to gain understanding, but I've learned that staying whole means I have to stop poking holes when God has spoken. If you are going to ask "why," first ask yourself why you need to know "why" so badly. Admit it- it is bondage. If the "why" is your struggle, I encourage you to view God's answer as a WHOLE answer. Once you've received His answer, one day at a time, practice not poking holes in what has been said.

Dear God,

Help me to value the time you have lent me. On this side of Heaven, please help me to prioritize acceptance of your answer to all of my questions, rather than prioritizing my expectation of why something is or isn't. I love you and I want to please you, but I admit that I have made the mistake of questioning your response. Help me to see what you draw in the picture, and not just stare for more hints about what is really there. Help me to accept what you say and see what you say as a whole answer. Help me Lord, not to put another question mark where you have put a period. Thank you for your patience with me as I learn to be at peace with what you do or do not say.

In Jesus' Name, Amen.

DAY 4

Psalms 1:1-3 NIV "Blessed is the one who does not walk in step with the wicked or stand in the way that sinners take or sit in the company of mockers, 2 but whose delight is in the law of the Lord, and who meditates on his Law Day and night. 3 That person is like a tree planted by streams of water, which yields its fruit in season and whose leaf does not wither – whatever they do prospers."

Ever heard the saying "Bad things happen to good people?" I've heard that one enough for all of us. The reality is that this is true. In life, sometimes, so called "bad" people seemingly commit horrendous deeds, and live life above the clouds. Then there are the "good" guys that just cannot catch a break. This is because the Word of God is true.

We are forewarned in Matthew 5:45 that God causes His sun to rise on the just and the unjust alike. Does that give us the all clear to live ratchet once we know right from wrong and are saved by grace? Nope! It is only by the Grace of God that those of us who have been saved are saved. Doing what is right is still the standard. Try not to get lost in the dizziness of comparison. Maintain a healthy acceptance of the biblical principle that the rain falls on the just *and* the unjust alike.

When you face life's obstacles, sometimes you have to encourage yourself. Always keep in mind that if it was too much for you, it would not be happening *to* you. You are built for this. Don't say to yourself "Why me?". Rather, say "Why not me?". Imagine yourself as a seed among millions of other seedlings. You have been planted in good soil. After the rains of life come pouring down, rejoice that you were not one of the seeds that got washed away or eaten with the worms. It is your birthright to sit in your emotions, but as Christians we have been born again. New birthright alert - don't be so consumed with the grief that you forget to celebrate the joy of being one of the seeds that remains. You are a survivor! Celebrate the fact that yet, you are still a growing tree; rooted and planted. And even when you are uprooted, you've still received the maximum benefit from the storm because now you have a testimony.

Once upon a time, you were a seed, but God kept you long enough for you to spring up. Yes, you may have lost a few branches but you are still who God created you to be. Who knows? Maybe you will get to inspire the next person by sharing your story. If trees could talk, they would have quite a story, wouldn't they? On this human journey, we transform constantly. I believe we are supposed to. After a few of your layers have dissipated, you may find your continued survival unlikely, but don't give up. Remember, God is a constant gardener. At the very least, celebrate the fact that you were sewn to grow.

Heavenly King,

In this abundant life which you have blessed me to live, please help me to accept that I will not be exempt from trials and tribulations. Since you are my provider, and you own everything, I trust that you will supply me with all that I need to survive. None of my storms are a surprise to you, so I praise you in advance for using the storms in my life to show me your power. With you, I am always victorious and prospering. Thank you for cleansing me with the waters of life, not to drown me, but to help me absorb from the storms what I need in order to grow.

In Jesus' Name, Amen.

DAY 5

1 Corinthians 13:4-8 NIV "4 Love is patient, love is kind. It does not envy, it does not boast, it is not proud. 5 It does not dishonor others, it is not self-seeking, it is not easily angered, it keeps no record of wrongs. 6 Love does not delight in evil but rejoices with the truth. It always protects, always trusts, always hopes, always perseveres. 8 Love never fails. But where there are prophesies, they will cease; where there are tongues, they will be stilled; where there is knowledge, it will pass away."

LOVE YOURSELF

Finding true love is an effort that may or may not be rewarded by humans, but God remembers and rewards our love journey. The key along such a journey, is to remember that God's definition of love outlines the keys to loving one another, as well as the keys to successfully loving ourselves. Self-love involves first recognizing that God loves you; you are lovable. As His children, we strive to be more like Him. This includes loving ourselves properly, because the love we so diligently search for can only start where us loving us begins.

As a child, my appearance used to be a major function and factor of my insecurities... especially my butt. Then, I grew up and had a "But GOD" moment. Now I love myself, flaws and all. Sometimes I'm harder on myself than others are; but at the end of the day, I love me because God is *in* me. If I overlooked loving myself and skipped right onto trying to love my neighbor, that would make little sense. You cannot nourish anyone on empty calories. Do I have insecurities? Sometimes. But only for a period of time. Just long enough for me to drag them jokers straight into my prayer time, and then they flee *over* time. The deeper insecurities- I know they are there, but I also believe that they are covered by the blood of Jesus.

Once you realize how much Christ loves us, you will realize that you have no excuse for failing to duplicate the same. So, just love. Constantly remind yourself that God created us and was pleased. That offers us the opportunity to be grateful for His love *and* to share it. Acknowledging the love of God also serves as a platform on which we can find appreciation for the differences of others, because He created them too! Accept His love. Healing the world begins with love. Love others, but definitely love yourself. You only get one life in the land of the living!

Lord,

Thank you for your unconditional love. Thank you also, for loving us enough to not only send us your salvation through your son Jesus, but for granting us access to the instructions for loving like you. This day, I admit that I have not loved you, myself, or others properly, and I give thanks to you for your grace that has covered me through my period of insufficiently loving. I now surrender my heart to you, and call into alignment, my ability to love. I decree that I will not try to take control with my own desires and carnality. Instead, I commit my will to love to you, so that you will love through me and be glorified and pleased. Lord, I am available to love, and be used to by love by you.

In Jesus' Name, Amen.

DAY 6

Habakkuk 2:2-3 NIV "2 Then the Lord replied: "Write down the revelation and make it plain on tablets so that a herald may run with it. 3 For the revelation awaits an appointed time; it speaks of the end and will not prove false. Though it linger, wait for it; it will certainly come and will not delay. "

WRITE IT DOWN

You ever read your diary from years ago or found a piece of paper with something you wrote on it? When you read what you wrote, I'm almost certain that a depiction of where you were and what the state of mind you were in at that specific time flashes through your mind. I've done this. When I look at my old prayer journals from childhood, I can still smell the food my mother was cooking on the stove when I was sitting in my room journalizing. If I read an entry from when I was grieving, I can feel that pain I was experiencing when I wrote that day. I can *see* what I was trying to say.

This is why I believe that we should never be too busy to write down your goals, even though it's true that goals change as we evolve and grow. Equally important, is journalizing your moments of gratitude about what God has done. Life happens, and you *may* forget them. If you or someone else finds them written down, the written thoughts will serve to remind you of how far you've come. Or, maybe what you've written will inspire and encourage someone else.

God has done amazing things through and for you, and He has use for your testimony. So, write the vision. Most importantly, write it unto God. Write as much as you can perceive. Write down every single great thing you learned from what you went through, and journalize what motivates you. Who knows? One day you may be inspired to act on a dream you journalized years before. Once you learn to acknowledge what inspires you, no one will be able to discourage you again. If you can perceive it, God can exceed it. You've heard it before, but listen again: Write the vision.

God,

Please help me to see what you say. Grant me serenity to accept not only what I cannot change, but also what you show me. Sometimes, what you place on my heart to do feels overwhelming, but because YOU are due all the glory, I am honored you have chosen me to carry it out. While I am on the grace-filled journey of salvation, please give me the discipline of documentation. Remind me of moments when your revelation visited me. Show me how YOU in Your power, through us, have the power to give your vision a voice and bring it to life.

In Jesus' Name, Amen.

DAY 7

2 Corinthians 6:14 NIV "Do not be yoked together with unbelievers. For what do righteousness and wickedness have in common? Or what fellowship can light have with darkness?"

Being single is not a curse. Likewise, being single *and* saved does not have to be boring. Although the bible says two is better than one (Ecclesiastes 4:9), there are things that God has planned for us to accomplish *while* we are single. In that regard, you can and should enjoy life no matter what your marital status is. Pamper yourself or an elderly relative. Volunteer your time at a nearby shelter. Go see a movie or take a mini staycation by yourself. All of the above build character, expose you to different cultures, and as an added bonus you'll create some new memories.

You don't have to mosey around or settle into an unfulfilling relationship just because you are single. The idea is to remember that you are whole, with or without a significant other. But, if you must date, and if you must mingle, it is important to date and mingle with proper purpose. First of all, if yours and your significant others' end-goals for dating don't match, you are possibly wasting your time. Yes, learning what you prefer in a mate is important, but it's not an excuse for blessing blocking. If you can't talk with them about Jesus, and you consider them a prime candidate for a spouse- something is off.

Too often, we do the same thing in different dating situations, which is insanity. Starting today, use what you know and stop using what isn't working. To get what you've never had, you have to do something you've never done. We have all heard that before, and it's true. Dating is not exempt. It is nothing more than data collection over a period of time, for your benefit, done by you. Nothing more unless you approve. Nothing less unless you don't! And, according to the bible, dating has a purpose: Marriage!!!

1 Corinthians 7: 8-9 NIV says "8 Now to the unmarried and the widows I say: It is good for them to stay unmarried, as I do. 9 But if they cannot control themselves, they should marry, for it is better to marry than to burn with passion." So, dating has an end goal: marriage. Likewise, the bible tells us in 1 Corinthians 7:2 NIV "But since sexual immorality is occurring, each man should have sexual relations with his own wife, and each woman with her own husband." Therefore, the place for *sex* is marriage. Not relationships, not courtships, not friendships. Marriage!

If you don't plan to marry, then don't date. And, if you aren't married, then you aren't supposed to be having sex. Period. God's word gives us boundaries to protect us. Case and point: Never send your body where you haven't first sent your mind. When you are not *interested* in marriage, seek God about what He desires for you to be focused on in that season. Don't get caught up in worldly standards and norms.

The pressure of fitting in can be overwhelming and can come from unexpected sources. I'm sure that people don't mean to provoke an unmarried woman to fornicate when they ask "When are you going to settle down or have a baby?", but that question is loaded. The pressure to reproduce and be in a relationship is heavy and unyielding. In my experience, it always led to me being focusing on the fact that I was single and childless. I wanted to be married and I wanted children, and those questions distracted me from the mode of acceptance that it just wasn't my time to experience either of the two yet.

The more the questions flooded in, the more I felt judged for being unmarried and childless. I got to a place where I just wanted to go get pregnant, not married, and have a baby simply to throttle the questions and the resulting feeling of inadequacy. That misapplied focus on worldly standards lead to lowered dating standards, detracted self-worth, disappointing dating experiences, unnecessary emotional scaring, and heavy BAGGAGE. Don't let anyone stir you to step outside of God's will. God created us and the mate He has for us, *if* He has a mate for us. That's right- some people will not ever be married. This is why it is important that we maintain a healthy understanding of God's purpose for the marriage covenant. Marriage is ministry, and not all of us are called to it. However, God has use for each of us either way.

As His child, learn respect His boundaries and trust His timing. Or, brace yourself for the repercussions of deciding to do it your way- sacrificing more than you have to and losing what you cannot replace. Date according to Gods principles, and you will be able to enjoy the roses (blessings) along the way. The roses give us stamina. Those moments when you realize that a past relationship was toxic and say to yourself "Thank God so-and-so left me", *those* are the roses my good people.

Success in the dating game is not equated by how successful you are at benefiting in ways that please the flesh (hotline blinging, DM's lit, current relationship convenience, etc.). Pleasing the flesh is simply a temporary island of relief, and if you are not careful, you will find yourself off outside of the will of God. As equally tragic as finding yourself outside of the will of God, is when you realize that on your path of self-pleasure, you've also lured others outside of the will God has for their life.

Yes, His grace is sufficient, but it is our responsibility to do right once we know the right thing to do. So, date wise. Seek the truth about the connections you have. Ask God to show you the reason the potential mate came into your life and wait for him to show you. Test the vibes without testing the sex.

Preserve your purity even though it is difficult and 110% unpopular. It is never too late to do that! Strive to see if you and your prospective mate share core values, beliefs, and interest. Take your time and remember that you are accountable to God for remaining pure. The person you may be dating cannot save you from the lake of fire, which is hotter than the heat of the moment that the devil will try to trip you up with. It. Is. That. Simple. You have the power.

Father God,

As I come to you with an honest and humble heart right now, I ask that you create in me a heart to seek you in all things first. I am aware that I am accountable to you for all that you bless me with, including my relationships with potential spouses. Please protect my mind and heart while I am collecting information about any person who I may ever date. Please don't allow the devil to trick me into believing that I know more than you. Help me to discern what is within, despite the outward representation.

I need your discernment because I am representing you in the dating process, and I do not want my conduct to lead others outside of your will. Please give me strength to peacefully accept when it is time to date or when is simply my time of divine development. I want the mate you have for me, but I accept that I may never be married and ask for the strength to be faithful to you even as a single believer.

Help me to release what is not mines. Every opportunity for fellowship and prayer that is presented to me in the form of a potential mate, give me self-control so that I proceed appropriately; in ways pleasing to you. I trust you for my spouse, but even if it is your will that I serve you singularly through life, I ask you to grant me the tenacity to STILL trust and obey you. Thank you for your grace and peace through the process of bringing me and my mate together if your will is for me to be made one flesh with a mate through marriage. And thank you for the peace and acceptance that I need if your will is for me to be committed whole-heartedly by myself in this life.

In Jesus' name. Amen.

DAY 8

Psalm 121:2 NIV "2 My help cometh from the Lord, the Maker of heaven and earth."

GODFIDENCE IS KEY

I once heard that confidence is the ability to stroll pass a pack of haters unaffected; that by having an "unbothered" attitude in a room full of opposers, *you* are the champion/ victor. I totally agree that we should demonstrate resilience in front of others whenever possible; adversaries included. However, it also very important that we openly acknowledge who the true source of our confidence and resilience is. Instead of having a "crabs in a bucket" philosophy in life, where as long as others are not superseding your success, you are content with life, boast about your confidence in God's ability to raise you up in due season (Galatians 6:9-10 NIV). Challenge yourself to use that same confidence in God to uplift others as well.

Being able to serve the only true God, is where my confidence is rooted. That is why I am "Peachy", rain or shine. I am fully persuaded that putting my trust in Him places me in line for His abundance. We are all first to God. He is the source of all of our resources, including our confidence.

Becoming successful but failing to share the true "secret" behind it is prideful and vain. Since we know that pride and vanity lead to destruction, the reality, no matter how cliché it sounds, is to share that God is the reason for our good success. So, remember to have Godfidence. Believe that all good things have come and will come from God. Sorry to be the one to break it to you, but, "You don't look like what you have been through" is truly a compliment to GOD; not us. Don't just be unbothered and bask in others acknowledgement that there is "something about you". While you have their attention, share the reason why you are so blessed. Lead a Godfident life.

Dear God,

*Thank you for the confidence that you have given me. True
confidence comes from you, and knowing who I am in you. Help
me to live confident in you; believing and trusting that you will
supply all of my needs. Help me to be content and grateful for
each day and all that is in it, even when it may be difficult to
conceive. Your word says that in my weakness, you are strong.
So, help me to remember to give you the credit for all of my
good success. Help me also, to believe you for the best
outcome, even in life's challenging situations. I want to inspire
others, not oppress them. You love us all, and I want to love like
you. You are the reason for every good and perfect thing. I
declare that I shall have every good and perfect thing you have
for me. I have unwavering confidence that you will provide.*

In Jesus' Name, Amen.

DAY 9

*Jerimiah 29:11 NIV "11 For I know the plans I have for you,"
declares the Lord, "plans to prosper you, plans to give you hope
and a future."*

LORD KNOWS...

In case you haven't received the profound revelation that God orchestrated the "it" before you knew about it, let me be the first to share with you: God knows. He knew you would cry about that guy, so he put so many red flags into play when you guys were "just hanging out." He knew you wouldn't get the promotion, so He created the job that you now have and have unexpectedly grown to love. You know, the one you always say feels like it was made for *just* for you.

Never confuse your timing with God's schedule. His is set in stone. His is divine. His plan is why all things work together for the good of those who love Him. Your job is to surrender and yield. The sooner you do so, the sooner you will enjoy the now for the now. The future is not held by any of us. It is created and controlled by God. We simply strap in for the ride. Learn to let God's promise sink in. Release all imaginations that don't line up with His word, and cast away every fear aside from reverence for Him. Be adjusted. Be encouraged. Be reminded that He has the best thoughts toward you and plans toward you. Relax.

Dear God,

I hear you today. I will listen intently for your instructions. And I'm not scared.

In Jesus' Name, Amen.

DAY 10

Romans 8:28 NIV "28 And we know that in all things God works for the good of those who love him, who have been called according to his purpose."

That both hands up emoji never leaves my emoji dashboard. God is just *that* good to me. I mean, just the fact that He is God, and he allows me the function of my brain on a daily basis? Mmm, Yea. Pretty sure that is why the both hands up emoji resonates strongly with me. Raise both hands if you've discovered that God can use a pandemic to accelerate your blessings. Raise both hands if God has kept you from harm and given you good vibes when you needed them most. Even what seems hard now will one day in hindsight be laughable. Why? You ask? Not because you are insensitive, but because NOTHING you go through was created to destroy you. However, it *may* even have been to destroy something about you that God never intended to be there, because God uses the things that make us most uncomfortable to prune us to perfection.

Every affliction you endure in this life will serve as evidence of Gods power, love, grace, mercy, and omnipotence. Live long enough, and you'll discover that the highest hurdles of growth for you produced some of the best characteristics *in* you. Possibly, they brought you closer to God and refreshed your spiritual senses. There isn't anything fresher than a new perspective. Pain is viewed in present tense; joy, just the same. In this human journey, you will experience varying degrees of both, but they cannot coexist. Just like fear and love- you can't have it both ways. The revelation is that God's word gives us power over pain and offers us the posture of unspeakable joy. Now THAT is a revelation worth both hands raised in total praise!

Dear God,

I come to you boldly with praise- Both hands up! I surrender and agree to walk as you have called me to walk- with a humble and grateful heart. Thank you for allowing me this opportunity to laugh in the devil's face. Although he thought he had my mind, you gave me peace. I may have flinched at the idea of defeat, but your word in Romans 8:28 gives me confirmation. You've officially affirmed that I will be victorious because I love you. I trust that you are at work in me and for me, for your purpose. I pray that my crushing brings glory to your name. You really are a good God. Thank You Father.

In Jesus' Name, Amen.

DAY 11

1 Thessalonians 5:16-18 NIV "16 Rejoice always, 17 pray continually, 18 give thanks in all circumstances; for this is God's will for you in Christ."

PRAY

It is ALWAYS time to pray. Pray for yourself. Pray for the lost. Pray even, for the stamina of the saved. Pray for the sick. Pray for the broken. Learn to name your past afflictions so that you can pray for others who may be struggling through them currently. Pray for leaders in every capacity across the world. Pray for the wicked and those who hate you. Pray for revelation and discernment. Pray for your family and friends. Pray for that stranger and that one-hit-wonder whose song you blasted, but now no one knows where they are; they may be struggling. Pray! Pray for the hungry. Pray for the victim and the criminal. Pray for a fresh anointing. Pray for strength. Pray for your pastoral and church family. Pray always for the body of Christ. Pray for your children and their future spouses. We should ALWAYS be in prayer.

Prayer time should be among your priorities. I can only lead by example with this one. Prayer is dialogue. If I had to define it, I'd say that for me, prayer is the constant yet intentional private, and sometimes public profession of the cares and affirmations of my heart, to God. BUT I will tell you that sometimes prayer is stillness and quietness in God's presence. Occasionally, my prayer time involves me waiting silently to hear from God. There may come time when *you* don't have the capacity to vocalize your prayers. I've been there. That's not a problem too hard for God because He hears your thoughts! One of the best feelings is that euphoria we experience after a conversation with the Lord. If you are struggling with prayer, it's okay. We have all been there or will be at some point. Guess what? It's okay to be silent before The Lord. Just make sure you don't forget to set aside time for Him.

When I'm struggling with what to say to God, I use a tried and true prayer model which begins with *praise* to God for what He has already done. Next, I *repent* for my iniquities and sins, and agree to turn to Him. Following that, I *acknowledge* that He is God and that I need Him. Finally, I *yield* to His will. Imagine if you prayed as much as you gossip. Imagine if you prayed as much as you cuss. Just imagine if you constantly prayed.

Dear God,

Thank you for waking me up this morning with new mercies and new opportunities to praise you. God, please forgive me for my iniquities against you; whether in fashion of commission or omission. I forgive and release my transgressors of the wrongs they've done against me. 1 Thessalonians 5:17 NIV advises me to "pray continually". As I come into agreement with your word, and commit to speak to you first about my needs, wants and cares, I lift up praises for what you've already done. I yield to your will for my life without looking back, unless it is to consider the many blessings you've bestowed upon me, and your grace.

In Jesus' Name, Amen.

DAY 12

2 Timothy 2:15 NIV "Do your best to present yourself to God as one approved, a worker who does not need to be ashamed and who correctly handles the word of truth."

ACCEPT THE TRUTH

If you cannot acknowledge the completeness implicated by the truth- you are in trouble. The truth stands alone boldly and sometimes it hurts. Trust me, I was crushed and embarrassed one night when I realized that I didn't actually know off hand what testament the book of Timothy was in. I was in my She-Room ALONE (lol), but it was still embarrassing. One, because I grew up in the church, and two - I study the word every day. The reality: I could have wasted so much time and flipped through the whole bible with a façade of expertise about the location of Timothy, but I simply went to the table of contents and looked it up. It was humbling, but I'm grateful that in that moment I learned how trusting in familiarity can trip me up.

This happens to us all; we all think we know something that we actually do not know *sometimes*. The real test is what do we do about it? For me, the answer has become: admit it. That's right. The sooner I learned to acknowledge the truth, the sooner I gained understanding and clarification. In that moment, the truth was that I didn't know the answer. I literally had a pop quiz on character when no one was watching. I had to get to a place where I didn't care who was watching. At this juncture, if the pastor say turn to the book of "so and so" and I don't know where it is, I will gladly flip to the table of contents lol. I refuse to act like I know it all because that is simply untrue.

The best thing you can do with the truth is swallow it, let it get into you, and accept it. Welcome it. Repeat it. Use it. The worst thing you can do to it is try to bend it or reshape it. And the worlds most added thing to the truth is OPINION!!! Everybody loves to add their two cents to the truth every now and again. It just feels better to do that sometimes.

The sobering agent between the truth and a lie is liberty. A lie will always make you feel like you have to keep lying. For whatever reason, when we lie, it's not unusual to feel a lascivious urge to do it again. That's because lying is bondage. Alternatively, the truth is solid ground. Embracing truth is a virtue. It's important to edify your spirit with truthful narratives. The truth will not rob you of your peace, and if you are struggling to accept a certain truth about yourself, others, or anything, just remember that God can handle it!

When it's too much, turn it over. Rather than toting around a pack of lies, drop the dead weight. You will instantly feel free. No matter how ugly the truth feels, I can testify that God WILL give you beauty for EVERY single ash. And as an added bonus, you get liberty. Now, who would say no to that?

Dear God,

This very world I live in sells me a lie on a constant basis, but I am so grateful for your truth, which you have made available to us in your word. Right now, I confess that whether intentionally or unintentionally – I have told a lie, accepted a lie, and at some point, lived a lie. But I ask that you would have mercy on me, and deliver me from our sinful nature. Lord please crush every untruth that I have carried in my spirit. Help me to lean on you for understanding and trust you for the capacity to embrace every truth presented to us no matter how challenging it may be. Encourage my spirit so that I will always be able to handle and prefer the truth over a lying spirit. Keep my conscious clean, God. I know people are watching and I pray you help me to not misrepresent you.

In Jesus' Name, Amen.

DAY 13

Galatians 6:9 NIV "Let us not become weary in doing good, for at the proper time we will reap a harvest if we do not give up. "

What's the first thing that runs through your mind when what you *want* to happen doesn't? When things don't turn out as you expected? When the relationship you so cherished ends, your job lays you off or overlooks you for the position you qualified for, dysfunction supersedes peace in your family, the disease isn't curable, or the pastor selects the other person as his armorbearer? For moments that bring about unsettled feelings and disappointment and shame, it is our duty to have an attitude of gratitude.

I know it sounds crazy, but guess what, it could be worse. For somebody you don't know, it *is* worse. When we a face life's obstacles, the first thing to remember is: you are built for this. This is your life and each of us only pass through here once. After you have realized that what you are experiencing is not defeating, allow yourself to accept all of the emotions that attempted to sweep you off base. Next, sit with those emotions.

See, obstacles come to you because you are alive, and since you are alive you have to face them. Your emotions are simply a signal that you still like or dislike something; that it still has the ability to impact and stir you in one way or another. You aren't supposed to get stuck there. Can you imagine always grieving, or always laughing, or always crying, or always feeling angry? It's a pattern of pure insanity, right? That's because what doesn't kill us, and what doesn't stop us (even those things that have the power to), are meant to propel us into greatness.

As long as you plan to live, you should expect to be challenged and to ultimately always overcome. If you are generous enough to consider that even your life is not all about you, you may also even inspire others to overcome as well. Plenty folk failed at inventions, 3-pointers, job interviews. For some of us we feel we've failed in relationships or even parenthood, but I believe that God uses our regrets and failures. Every day is a new chance to win. The blessing is that if you keep going, you will experience the opposite of failure.

Don't let your mind get stuck in a season that God has delivered you out of. Yes, life will knock you down sometimes. Yes, you will feel like damaged goods after the big battles. The blessing is that what came at you only knocked you down; you are still alive and you can still get up. Cling to your Rhema Word- that promising revelation that God has spoken to you. Hang in here!

Heavenly Father,

I come to you humbly asking you to grant me tenacity and strength to fight the good fight in this life. I declare that I am an overcomer. In the midst of my storms, please always give me your peace. Help me to hear your voice when life's problems seem so loud. Give me a Rhema Word that will carry me in times of hardship. Remind me of who I am so that I don't take on a false and feeble identity out of convenience.

Your word exemplifies perseverance, rather than cowering or giving up. I need you to reign down your supernatural stamina upon me so that I can get to where you have created me to go. I proclaim in Jesus name that I will do all you have created me to do. I will have all you have created me to have. I will be all that you have created me to be. Even if I fail at something, I will get up and try again. Even in the face of adversity, I will overcome. For your glory always, Father.

In Jesus' Name, Amen.

DAY 14

1 Peter 2:9 NIV "But you are a chosen people, a royal priesthood, a holy nation, God's special possession, that you may declare the praises of him who called you out of darkness into the marvelous light"

BE YOU

If you don't find the courage to be anything, at least be brave enough to be yourself. I mean your real self. Stop spoofing people. When you commit to being somebody you are not, you catfish others and yourself. The devil loves to disparage us. He'll make you feel validated when you display your alter ego, and then tell you that you aren't worthy of being yourself behind closed doors. Just remember, if anybody is worthy of being you, it is YOU.

There is no need to hide your deficiencies because we all have them. We are all very proficient is some areas and not so proficient in other ones. Invoke laughter if your strength is comedy. Heal if you are always feeling lead to lend kind words. Motivate if you have too much energy for *just* you. If you aren't the talking type, make sure your words count. Don't be ashamed to share who you are for fear of rejection or being a misfit.

When I was a teenager, my teacher went around the room telling each student one thing she had learned about each of us. When she got to me, she said "you will never fit in." I laughed at what she said right along with everyone else, but truthfully, in that moment I was ashamed. Mainly because deep down, I knew she said something about me that I had always tried to mask. I had always felt it, and I did everything up until that point to "fit in." In hindsight, what she said should have affirmed me. The bible says in 1 Peter 2:9 that we are a peculiar people. I just didn't realize that even at such a young age I was exuding one of the main characteristics of being a child of God. The trick of the enemy is always to confuse you about who you are so that you won't reach your full potential. Looking back, I am so grateful that I have never fit in. Maybe I never will.

At this point, I wouldn't mind. Listen, not every crowd will be for you, and not everyone will understand you, but your light will brighten the way for those who it is supposed to. Being embarrassed is not worse than being misunderstood, so don't you ever hold back your true identity. I'm not saying be ruthless. I'm saying be 100% authentic at all times. You have to let your guard down with someone. More important is that you let your guard down *after* you let JESUS in. That way, when the war begins you've already won.

Say what you need to say because "you've got to do what you got to do." Who decides what you wear, my darling, if you don't? God!!! And it isn't clothes, it is you! In other words, dress in you every day. Put on the full armor of God (Ephesians 6:10-18) first, but don't forget to nurture the YOU underneath it. As you know, everybody else is taken and they always will be. So that leaves you no choice. You've got to be you. Period.

Lord,

Thank you for taking the time to create me. You don't make mistakes, and you were pleased with what you made when you formed me. Therefore, I will be, also. Through Christ, all things are possible. That means I can be myself even though I have imperfections. Since you are perfect, I ask that you constantly rub off on me. Shine me up with your truth and peace. Help me to appreciate what you installed in me so that I will able to minister to myself and others appropriately. As you renew my mind, help me to accept and love myself. Help me to bring my cares to you and affirm me so that I will not drown in insecurity.

In Jesus' Name, Amen.

DAY 15

Matthew 7:7 NIV "Ask and it will be given to you; seek and you will find; knock and the door will be opened to you."

FINDERS KEEPERS

It is so easy to get lost in all the false narratives about who we should be, but by any means necessary, find yourself. After you do that, find out what it is you love doing and never stop. No one can take what you know away from you. That's what makes education so valuable. Knowledge is power. What you love doing is your equalizer and it is also the passion you have been thriving off of your whole existence. If you don't feel passionate about anything in particular, try doing something outside of your comfort zone. I'm not saying do something that will draw you outside of the faith or endanger yours or the life of others, just encouraging you to explore the possibilities. Stay before the Lord about what your calling is and your purpose will follow not too far behind. You will only see as far as you believe you can see. And again, I say, find yourself.

Dear God,

Please help me to always seek your guidance and your approval regarding my choices. Thank you for the freedom to ask anything of you. Thank you for the reassurance that my enlightenment matters to you. Thank you for affirming that you have a divine purpose for all that I know and will ever learn. As I journey through life, help me to discover what you want me to know. I appreciate your grace and mercy and patience towards me while I process the wisdom you grant me. Please properly align my passions and curiosities with your will, and keep me in your perfect peace.

In Jesus' Name, Amen.

DAY 16

Romans 12:2 NIV "2 Do not conform to the patterns of this world, but be transformed by the renewing of your mind. Then you will be able to test and approve what Gods will is – his good, pleasing, and perfect will."

BE AUTHENTIC

This applies with everyone, not just with the ones you love. And it's not just about honesty. It's also about charity. It's about coming to the table and leaving it all there. It's about leading by example, proactively. It's about treating people how you want to be treated and showing people how you expect to be treated. Stop walking around like you are sworn to secrecy about your truth. Wear it even if you know it's unappealing. By doing so you'll encourage others to do the same. You'll also create value, and without forcing it, subtly command an appreciation for who you *really* are. Being forthcoming is about being okay with the nay-sayers checking out. Yes, the truth hurts, but your truth can't be embraced without first being accepted by you.

Lord,

I am doing my best to imitate you. Dwell in my spirit and soul. Don't let the darkness of this world and its false narratives overshadow your purpose for me. Shine in me so that I may see what is inside of me and value it. Help me to nurture the seeds you plant in me so that I can grow. Give me your presence so that I can stand. Hold me up so that I will always be whole.

Remind me of what you promised me when I am tempted to take on someone else's identity. Everything around me is ever changing and I don't want to get caught up with trying to "keep up with the Joneses". Please give me the confidence to be myself. You have specifically anointed me to do so. You have given me the unique opportunity to represent you like only I can. You have given me several gifts which I can use to glorify you. Since I am your vessel, I ask that you increase in me and use me freely. In your way, let my existence be ministry, and give me the courage to be who I am so that you can use me. Thank you for choosing me.

In Jesus' Name, Amen.

DAY 17

Ecclesiastes 3:1 NIV "There is a time for everything, and a season for every activity under the heavens:"

YOU ARE RIGHT ON TIME

Did you know that some rainbows come out at night? Does this mean they aren't rainbows? No! They are still beautiful, and they are still rainbows. What makes a daytime rainbow different from a night one? The sun and the moon! Two very different planets, yet they still have the capacity to produce something so profound; each of them in their own time. You see, we cannot get the days back, but we can learn to shine when it is our time. Even if our time is not when we expect.

Years ago, in a rush, I went to a nail salon that I typically wouldn't patronize, *especially* at night. I'd accepted a last-minute dinner invitation and wanted to get dolled up for the occasion. However, by the time my nails were done, I decided it was too late to dine out. So, I accepted the pedicure offered at the end of my nail service. Just before the technician finished my pedicure, an elderly woman was seated next to me. She never said a word until I got up to leave.

Just as I arose to exit the salon, she said "You can never run faster than your angels can fly." I was immediately creeped out. Mainly because I didn't know who she was speaking to. Then, she said it again: "Young lady, I don't know you but I need to tell you to slow down. You can't outrun your angels." In that season of my life, I interpreted what she said as "walk it out." However, I constantly revisit that wisdom, and it serves me well in many ways as I journey through the varying stages of human life. That very nugget of wisdom helps me to slow down and regain pace when my speed trips me up.

Rushing is a lot like blowing the fire out of lit candles. Blow too hard and you might get burned. Blow too light and you won't get results. If you *must* hurry, let it be to acquaint yourself with the virtue of patience. Some things happen in the blink of an eye, sure, but what about the things that are meant to be enjoyed? Ever look back and realize you missed the sweet spot? I have. When my son turned 3, I got a flashback of how he was much more dependent not too long ago. The flashback felt good, but the idea that in some ways, I wish time had moved a little slower. It would have been nice if I had enjoyed what was happening *when* it was happening, right?

Certain seasons of life might not feel so sweet while you are in them, but try to remember to take things one day at a time. Even in the hard times, there are still those uplifting moments that help us push through. If you are too preoccupied to savor those brief moments of relief, you'll look back one day with regret. The first step in divorcing regret is to live in the moment. Tomorrow is not promised to anyone.

So, forgive yourself for complaining because you are human!!! The good news is that the next thing smoking *is* your tomorrow, if you live to see it. Give thanks to God for another chance to get it right EVERYTIME you wake up on the other side of sleep! Even if you went to bed with a heavy heart last night, the gift in the grief is that you woke up today. You *can* choose today to pay attention to what's in front of you without losing sight of where you are headed. Rush through and you'll have to repeat the lesson all over again!

Dear God,

Thank you for your patience. Please share some of it with me. I don't want to make moves out of season, and I also don't want to miss a single revelation that you release to me. In this life, I am trusting you to keep all of your promises to me, but I dare not rush or hurry you. Sure, there are moments when I feel that things could go my way a little sooner, but you are always right on time. Thank you for every season you have blessed me to survive. Thank you for sending wisdom on a whim to rescue me from my anxieties. Thank you for allowing me to humble myself before life has to do it for me. I pray that you keep me from running to a location outside of your will, and continue to let me experience your perfect timing.

In Jesus' Name, Amen.

DAY 18

1 Peter 5:7 NIV "Cast all your anxiety on him because he cares for you."

SURRENDER

At all times, only God is in control. Even when things seem uncertain and unpredictable, you can rest assure that He never slumbers nor sleeps. For me, that means I don't have to lose sleep at night. What a relief! However, from time to time, human nature still tries to take the wheel. The good news is that God's nature *supersedes* human nature. So, we can trust that He is the best one to relinquish control unto. Besides, who wants to fight unnecessary battles? Even the easy fights add up.

Personally, I don't want to fight nobody over anything. I don't care if it's a parking space, the last laugh, the last word, the last jug of milk at the store, or a chair with MY name on it. No struggle is worth losing peace of mind. When I make decisions, I set a standard that I have to ask God first. Before I go to anyone, I go to him. Since I can't stand anxiety, my coping mechanism has become surrendering and letting go. If I catch myself worrying about the outcome of something, I stop and remind myself that it's not cancer and nobody died. Literally. Even when it *is* cancer, and even when somebody *does* die, I grieve and continue to maintain confidence that God is *still* God; He is still in total control, not me.

I'm not insensitive, but these days I don't do pity parties. They don't serve me. Ever since I survived that pulmonary embolism and Factor V diagnosis, the over analyzing and drawing conclusions thing- it's too expensive for me. I refuse to pay for worrying, *especially* now that I know the form of currency could potentially be my health. It took a near-death experience for me to realize how unnecessary having a controlling nature really is, but, I'm still grateful that I lived to receive the revelation that surrender is our only option. Refusing to surrender and yield to God's will is far too exhausting *and* it doesn't change anything. It's not always God's will for what we want to be what *is*. Sometimes, we fight so hard for a desired outcome that we actually forget the reason we want that result in the first place.

Repeat after me: Power belongs to God. Just because things don't always turn out how we intend them to, that doesn't mean God is punishing us. God would never abuse His power. He simply doesn't have to. So, the next time you feel that someone is getting the best of you, taking your kindness for weakness, remember who is fighting for you. Never change who you are to avoid losing control. It's not your job to control. It is your job to surrender constantly and let God do *His* job.

If you are kind, stay kind, because He can use your kindness. Yes, people will take advantage of it, but God will also reward you for your obedience. Stay on the straight and narrow. Never let a crooked smile deter you from keeping a straight face. Remain solid, flaws and all. Remember who's you are. Otherwise, you'll always be nursing new wounds. Let go and let God.

Dear God,

I simply surrender. You don't need my permission to do what you are going to do. You are God all by yourself. I yield to your will. Humbly, I pray for your forgiveness for trying to do things according to my agenda. I accept your agenda and ask for your permission to be included in your great work. Please free me from the bondage of the need to control everything. I believe that the life you have for me is so much better that anything I could orchestrate, and I trust YOUR manifestation will always be sufficient.

In Jesus' Name, Amen.

DAY 19

1 Thessalonians 5:12 NIV "Now we ask you, brothers and sisters, to acknowledge those who work hard among you, who care for you in the Lord and who admonish you."

COMMAND APPRECIATION, NOT TOLERANCE

Thanks, but no thanks- the best thing you can say to anything that doesn't welcome you. Everything is not a battle, which is why I don't only have "oh, hey" moments with people, I have "oh, bye" moments with them too. Seasons and reasons are real. Once you have been broken, it can feel so good to be received. It's so uplifting to be tolerated, when you feel like you are in pieces. However, I challenge you to see yourself as whole and command appreciation. No matter what.

When someone receives you after you've been broken, remind yourself that by showing up- you have already done your hard work. Otherwise, you enforce a code of silence onto yourself and you won't be open to receive what they have to offer you. There is an abundance of love still existing in this land of the living. Try not to count yourself out so much. God's grace is not up to you; therefore, you shouldn't be in pursuit of it. It cannot be earned. That's what makes Him, God.

Imagine if you saw yourself as He sees you. That's really what makes the difference. That *is* the secret to wholeness. Dig into Ephesians and Psalms. Learn who you are so that you can confidently command the appreciation of who God created you to be. The healthy humility necessary to ward of a proud spirit comes from recognizing that God's Grace is so great that we cannot earn it. Therefore, since grace comes from Him and we do not earn it, we should not be in pursuit of people's tolerance. We should be in pursuit of their appreciation. That's what facilitates witness opportunities.

We are everything to those who will recognize it. However, not everyone is meant to recognize the greatness in you. Some will see it and nurture; others will eyeball your fierceness a mile away and go out of their way to crush it. So, don't force it. Protect what is bestowed upon you by God, and pay attention for opportunities to share. Sharing is ministry, but only to those who find what you have to share "well received". Being sensitive to the Holy Spirit will enable you to minister appropriately to whom your ministry is meant to reach.

People can never be influenced by what they do not appreciate. So, it's not really too bad to be forgotten, if the people who lose memory of you never appreciated and cherished you in the first place. It's okay to detach with love. You are not giving up on them, you are blessing them to God. Maybe they are someone else's witness opportunity. Maybe not. Once God has released you to do so, release *them*. Refuse to tolerate a few crumbs of acceptance and demand the appreciation you deserve. It's as simple as that.

Dear God,

Thank you for your love and kindness. You sent your only begotten Son to die for me. That's how much I mean to you. Now that I have accepted Christ, He dwells inside me. I am not just a shell. I am a gift because my spirit has been enriched by the greatest gift – Jesus. In your way, help me to accept when I am not received. Free me from self-destructive strongholds. Encamp your angels around me to hold me up when I am feeling beat down by rejection. Fortify my spirit. Help me to property represent you.

I approach your throne boldly, asking for the permission to openly have joy, peace, intelligence, intuition, gifts, confidence, and every desire of my heart that you will. Let your omnipotence illuminate the dark places within me. Let every opportunity I have to witness to others for the salvation of their souls magnify and please you.

In Jesus Name, Amen.

DAY 20

Isaiah 41:10 NIV "So do not fear, for I am with you; do not be dismayed, for I am your God. I will strengthen you and help you; I will uphold you with my righteous right hand."

1 IS A WHOLE NUMBER

One thing for certain, all it takes is one. One bad apple. One good soul. No matter how you do the math, there is nothing insignificant about the quantity of one. Just because your marital status is single, doesn't mean you are alone. Single is not a number. Many people have been defeated by a force that they couldn't see. Just because you are alone don't mean you have to be a loner. Live free, laugh with someone you love about your conquests. You are not better to have been a loner that to not have been at all. Share yourself, your gifts, your ministry, your resources, your stories, your laughter. Be influential and remember that no matter who leaves our life, God is always with us. All it takes to create change is one encounter with The Lord.

Lord,

You sent your ONLY begotten son to die for my sins. He alone paid the price. You didn't need anyone else to volunteer or re-do what He did. The miracle of Christ exemplifies how you are able to use just one. You made your will perfect the first time. Because of you, I am complete. Because of you I am reconciled and made whole. Even with all my scars, you alone mend me up and keep me together. When I was single, you never left me by myself. Your Holy Spirit always comforted me. I pray that you visit every person who feels left behind. Remind them of your presence. For the people who sit among many yet experience loneliness, please fill every void and reaffirm your love toward them. Show yourself strong in us. While many may be by themselves, you are omnipotent and omnipresent. I might not be in the clique or crowd, but in your love, I am secure.

In Jesus' Name, Amen.

DAY 21

Romans 16:17-18 NIV "17 I urge you, brother and sisters, to watch out for those who cause divisions and put obstacles in your way that are contrary to the teaching you have learned. Keep away from them. 18 For such people are not serving our Lord Jesus Christ, but their own appetites. By smooth talk and flattery they deceive the minds of naïve people."

JUST LEAVE IT

It's difficult to let go of something you really care about when you don't have a replacement; another best friend, another boyfriend, another job. I've been in this situation more than a few times and the reality is that I was holding onto wasn't good for me. The lie at play when we face letting go is that it's better to keep what you have until you get what you need. It's not. When we try to drag something out or force something, we lose sight of the fact that God may have something better. In actuality, sometimes it's better to let go than to try to fix what's broken. This applies to relationships, jobs, and ideas to name a few.

Some things are solvable within our individual capacity, others are not. We must trust that what God has for us is not just for us, it is also what's *best* for us. I've discontinued pursuit of dreams that were near and dear to me. Sometimes for a season, and sometimes for good. The beautiful truth is that when I released those ideas to God, he either reassigned it to me with confirmation or replaced a good idea with a better one. Either way, the lesson is that holding onto it out of season was a hinderance.

Over the course of time, I've learned that God will not let something you need leave your life unless He is going to replace it with something better. Therefore, walk guilt-free in the freedom to leave anybody who treats you like a nobody, because you are already somebody to God. When a friendship has run its course, detach with love. Stop waiting until something chaotic is the reason you part ways. There is a season for everything. Letting go is not giving up, it *is* getting out of Gods way. In time, God will reveal His reason for giving you pause. Your job is to remain obedient.

God,

Thank you for your word. Every day I find another reason to get healthier inside and out. Sometimes that means you prune me and cause me to purge what I'm not ready to release, but I thank you for every resource you have provided unto me. You inspire me to always give my best. I dare not waste time. You are a faithful father, and you are kind enough to answer my call. As I learn the discipline of release, grant me your discernment so that I know when to let go. Everything I have, you have given me, and everything I will ever have is what you intend to come to me. Help me to remember that what you have for me is for me. Give me confirmation when I need it so that I won't toil in grief for releasing what was never mines to keep. Thank you for making all things new and for always giving me better and best. May I always use the time you give me in the way you purpose. Let not one moment of my life be squandered by me doing anything or holding onto anything that gets in your way. Thy will be done in me.

In Jesus' Name, Amen.

DAY 22

Ephesians 4:2 NIV "Be completely humble and gentle; be patient, bearing with one another in love."

STAND BY

Repeat after me: I will always be young in the right places. Aren't you glad you don't look like what you have been through? I personally believe that when we connect with Christ, we look even LESS like what we've been through. When you are born again, you are constantly putting on renewed everything – strength, thoughts, and intentions - hopefully. But there will be phases in life when your level of maturity exceeds that of someone older than you. I have experienced it many times. I mean, we have all probably sat and conversed with someone for a few moments, only to realize how regressive they are. Not from a judgmental standpoint, but just spiritually. They are 56, but their perspective and demeanor are 15. It can be so frustrating, right? Especially when that person has an authoritarian role on your job or in your family. How do you face them knowing that they are so underdeveloped? You give them grace! This is where humility comes in.

God stands by you while you mature; constantly giving you His grace. So, it's a small labor of love for you be patient towards others as well. You don't stress. Again, you surrender. Not to their will, but to God's, because he allowed your paths to cross for a reason. Focus on the lesson in it all and you'll notice that you are not as frustrated with the person. As Christians, we should hate the sin, not the person. Remember, we have all been promoted into positions that we are not qualified for. If you haven't yet, one day you will be. When it's your turn, you'll be glad for the patience and grace of others. It will grow you spiritually and I believe it is Christlike to be longsuffering.

Jesus knew Judas was going to betray him, but He still broke bread with him. The audacity to do what is right, even to someone that you don't necessarily agree with or that you are aware holds contempt for you, that is longsuffering. Stand in the gaps and pray. Do what Jesus would do.

Dear God,

Thank you for standing by me. You have been so gracious towards me. Even when I deserve harshness, you deal with me gently. Your patience towards me shows me how to be compassionate and patient with others. Many times, it shocks me when I encounter someone who is older than me, but less spiritually developed. Lord, make room in my heart for other people's immaturities and mistakes, just as I would want others to accommodate mines. Especially with my brothers and sisters in Christ, and even with those who haven't come to know you yet. Everywhere I go, I want to be able to stand supportively and interact appropriately with others, even when it feels like they are inconveniencing me. Help me to bear with others and be a team player.

In Jesus' Name, Amen.

DAY 23

Proverbs 18:20-21 NIV "20 From the fruit of their mouth a person's stomach is filled; with the harvest of their lips they are satisfied. 21 The tongue has the power of life and death, and those who love it eat its fruit."

MAKE YOUR DECLARATIONS

Declarations are one of the greatest weapons of spiritual warfare. I come up with new ones all the time. One of my favorites ones is from when I went through a traumatic experience with one of my relatives, but you don't have to wait until that happens to you. It is this: I declare, that I have no reason to let the negativity of others make me ungrateful to GOD. Not ever. I won't let it!

You can't control what others do and the truth is, most of the time, neither can they. What some fail to realize and make necessary to accept, is a truth signified in Ephesians 6:12 NIV: "For our struggle is not against flesh and blood, but against the rulers, against the authorities, against the powers of this dark world and against the spiritual forces of evil in the heavenly realms."

This life requires God, and I'm so grateful that I don't allow guilt to rise up inside of me for declining to get entangled in ungodly bondage. I declare that I am free forever. I declare that not one of my enemies will triumph over me. I could go on and on. I proclaim that I will praise the Lord. I declare that God will keep every promise he has made to me. I declare that I am who God says I am. Try it with me!!! We have far too many darts from hell trying to land in our laps, for us to be shy about what we believe.

Declarations are a defense mechanism. They can also serve as a gateway for dialogue with God when you don't know what to say to Him. Tell God what you know about him. The enemy hates when you know better. When the devil comes with his tricks and lies, declare that you have the power. Stop claiming that you are tired, bored, lonely, hungry, sad, and broke, or you may stay in those traps. Speak that your body is rested and call every function into alignment with the body of Christ.

Declare that your hands are anointed to do what God wants you to do. Proclaim that you are never alone because God is always with you. Instead of moping around with a defeated spirit, declare war on the enemy. You are an army of two: yourself, led by God. I make declarations aloud EVERY DAY. So much so, that my kids start declaring what I declare. It's a beautiful thing! God has given you dominion over everything on earth. Anything God provides is a terrible thing to waste.

Lord,

I first need to apologize for not using the power you've given me. You have given me the power, by faith, to move mountains. When I come to you, I believe you are listening and that you will answer. So, there is no reason for me to be neglectful. There are battles that you have equipped me to win, and I want to make you proud. I am your child; therefore, I lack nothing. You are inside of me, alive and well. Therefore, there is no way the enemy is going to get a leg up on me. I believe everything you said about me in your word. I am in this world but not of this world. I pray that you continue to hear my declarations and that they will always be in line with your divine operations.

In Jesus' Name, Amen.

DAY 24

1 Thessalonians 5:19-22 NIV "19 Do not quench the Spirit. 20 Do not treat prophecies with contempt, 21 but test them all; hold on to what is good, 22 reject every kind of evil."

ALWAYS TEST PERSPECTIVE

Some people will tell you "Life is too short." Don't believe them. The truth is that our lives are all predetermined by God. Life *is*, however, going to be long for some and short for others. It is not about how long or short you are here. There's more to life than just calculating the days. Although it's true that God knows the number of our days, no one else *except* Him knows. Not even the people who say "Life is too short." So, don't worry about the people living in a hurry, afraid they'll run out of time. Don't stop living long enough to listen to such foolery.

Don't allow anyone force their perspective on you. We all see things differently for a reason. You are not responsible for anyone's perspective but your own. Being influenced and being brainwashed are two different things. Don't mistake "Holy Roller Religious People" for the Holy Spirit. Don't waste the time people tell you to doing that you haven't checked out with God. Ask God for instruction. He will sometimes provide it through another person. But know this: it is healthy and right to test the spirit you encounter in others. Often times, people will tell you to do or don't do something they wouldn't even do themselves. Why go on a dummy mission? Do they know your story? Are they the author of your life? While we all play a valuable role in each other's life, sometimes we snag insignificant advice that does not lead to wisdom. Talk to God first. He may send your answer through another, but not always. Follow your God-breathed intuition. Note I said "God-breathed." Not feelings, emotions, or other people's advice under pressure.

Dear God,

Thank you for the diverse spectrum of personalities and perspectives which you have afforded me the opportunity to witness. Thank you also, for the ability to discern your voice so that I know what not to entertain. Help me to receive YOUR instruction despite the method of delivery. Thank you for your wisdom, which helps me to know how to receive edification from Godly sources. Show me who to trust. Position me to be a good steward of everything you bestow upon me. Please continue to give me instruction and help me to see the love you have for me, even in moments of correction.

In Jesus' Name, Amen.

DAY 25

1 Thessalonians 4:3-5 NIV "3 It is God's will that you should be sanctified: that you should avoid sexual immorality; that you should avoid sexual immorality; 4 that each of you should learn to control your own body in a way that is holy and honorable, 5 not in passionate lust like the pagans, who do not know God;"

Now, let me begin by saying that I was raised in the church, but I have not always been saved. Before I exercised authority over my flesh, I fell short and more times than a little bit. I was predisposed to sexual immorality as a child because I was sexually abused, but that is no excuse for some of the decisions I made once I arrived at an age of understanding. I have not always obeyed God's word regarding sex, but I feel it is still important for me to acknowledge that there is a standard.

The consequences of yielding to my flesh with my body, in a sexual manner, were deep and real, and it is best that I present to you the accurate account because I am in no ways perfect. I simply serve a perfect God, who I seek strength from on a consistent basis, in order that I remain fully delivered from the residue of sexual abuse as a child, and the yolk of biblically qualified sexual immorality as a young woman.

It's no surprise that many of us have the incorrect understanding of sex, because we live in a world that over-sensationalizes and over-sexualizes everything. However, sensual and sexual are not the same. Sensual has more to do with our feelings, and sex has more to do with our spirit. Why do you think sexual orgasms are likened to an out-of-body experience?

Sexual immorality is sold openly. You can find encouragement to participate in sexually immoral things on social media, in movies, and even in the church. Oops... Did I say church? Yup! You see, the church has no walls, it is built with the people for bricks. As followers of Christ, we are the church. Wherever we are, the church is there, and when we don't address sexual immorality in church, we simply welcome it in.

It's not uncommon to see your church buddies posting pictures of themselves at a concert supporting secular artists who promote promiscuity, adultery, or witchcraft. Happy Resurrection Sunday one day, and provocative post the next day. Ummhmm. If you've ever wondered how this happens, it's been happening since the first sin in the Garden of Eden. Once humanity sinned, we kept on sinning. Sexual immorality is just one way we do it, but we must remember that there are consequences for letting sexual immorality's foot in our doors.

The enemy is very subtle with his mechanisms of confusion, so it's always best to educate yourself. Learning what God says about sex is the very way to cancel confusion season when it comes to sex. The reason why it's important to know the difference is because there is an order of operation. You can have sex without being sensual, but enjoyable sex is sensual, but based on the bible, sex is for a man and his wife (1 Corinthians 7:2-5). Period. The pressure to have sex is so heavy in our society that some are literally just having sex JUST to have sex, but we must remember to cast down our sinful nature daily. Sex appeal exists for a reason. Sex exists for a reason. Sexiness exists for a reason. Sexuality exists for a reason. Don't let anyone exploit or over sensationalize your understanding of sex.

God created sex, and He didn't create it for premarital, recreational use. He is far too intentional for that. So, before you sexualize, familiarize. Prematurely engaging in sex can produce catastrophic consequences. Among them are sexually transmitted diseases (STDs) and spiritually transmitted spiritual strongholds (STSS) aka soul ties.

STDs can kill you, and even if you live to talk about it, they can rob you of your ability to reproduce. They can alter your health forever. A few minutes of pleasure is not worth risking your quality of life permanently. Today, many STDs are curable, but that doesn't mean you should engage in the ultimate way to prevent them- Abstinence. Abstinence is abstaining or refraining from all sexual activities until marriage.

I was abstinent for nearly 2 years before I got married. I can tell you that I was tempted to have sex and engage in sexually immoral behavior far more once I committed to abstaining from sex until marriage. After I entered into a purity covenant, and especially once I met my husband, the struggle to be loyal to my decision to abstain was even harder. Mainly because I had already engaged in fornication before making the commitment to abstain, but also because of the spiritual warfare that follows any willful commitment to Godly directives.

What helped me was that I held onto a Rhema Word that I received from a homeless woman years prior (when I was totally not abstinent lol). She walked through the barbershop as I was waiting my turn for an eyebrow appointment and spoke a word to me that I believe was from God because it actually came to fruition. As she walked by dragging herself one leg at a time, slurring words and chuckling at herself as she spoke, she went down the line – proclaiming things over each patron; one seat at a time.

When she got to me, she said "Aww, Honey! You going get a good man! Ummhmm, and you not going to have to take no trips to the bedroom to get him. Nope. And he sure going to love you!!" Then, on to the next person she went. Most of us there gave her a donation, but I did so grudgingly because I was annoyed. I was actually *there* with my significant other. The same significant other who would later lock me in his room, choke me until I was unconscious, rape me as I regained consciousness, hold me captive for nearly 24-hours, and FINALLY escort me to the emergency room, but only because I started hemorrhaging. All that, and BOOM- I got hit by a truck in the hospital parking lot on the way into ER.

I mean, this was a guy who never had to beg me for sex. He was also a man who was secretly using drugs. The rage that came out the night he raped me? Well, let's just say I've come to realize that I had no business with him in the first place. I had all the signs that he didn't love me and was NOT dating for marriage, despite him being a preacher's kid. The fornication that I willingly participated in, opened the door for every demonic STSS and ultimately lead to the rape incident. Healing from that relationship and the trauma of being raped took years of therapy and spiritual deliverance.

Any who, the homeless lady was correct, just 10 years early. She was warning me, and I wasn't ready for what she said because I was still blinded by the strongholds of my then relationship. STSSs are the spiritual urges and desires that are transmitted between two people who engage in sex. It happens when any form of sex is practiced. In a marriage, you agree to receive STSSs when you take your sacred vows before God and your loved ones.

Outside of the marriage covenant, you basically blindly sign up to receive every spiritual urge and desire the person you sleep with has. That could be many things- addiction, promiscuity, lasciviousness, joy, and despair. Not all STSSs are bad, but why disobey God and blindsight yourself? I believe that God chastens whom he loves. When we make the decision to disobey him, especially with our bodies (his earthly dwelling place), we risk stepping into the devil's playground and outside of His will. What a good God he is, that he would put roadblocks in front of us, to keep us from enjoying disobedience enough to stay in it.

Just know that if you have sex outside of the marriage covenant, God forgives. You do not have to suffer with guilt for your past after repentance. The bible says in Romans 8:1 NIV: "Therefore, there is now no condemnation for those who are in Christ Jesus". So, don't beat yourself up. With all that said, stay on the straight and narrow. Don't buy into the "if you can't beat em, join em" philosophy when it comes to sex. Don't allow sexiness, sex, sex appeal, and sexuality to catch you off guard. Stand for something, or you will fall for anything.

Lord,

Your grace is sufficient. This applies to all areas of my life and every mistake. I admit that I am guilty of yielding to my flesh sexually, sometimes even acting it out. The spiritual and physical consequences are heavy, but I ask that you lift the guilt and shame from me now. Rebuke sexual immorality for my sake. I pray that everyone suffering from the shame and loneliness of contracting a sexually transmitted demonic spirit, an unplanned parenthood, or even a sexually transmitted disease will receive your forgiveness, deliverance, and peace.

For every person who has been sexually violated, I pray that you will heal and restore them. Give them the liberty and joy again that only you can. Surround them with the support they need. Thank you for the survivors of sexual abuse and immorality. Thank you for your deliverance from every unclean spirit and for breaking of every ungodly stronghold. You make no mistakes, despite the error in our ways. Give me the tenacity to abstain from premarital sexual encounters. I believe that in you I can have a fresh start. Only you can carry me through my temptations to the way of escape. Help me to always escape the entanglement of all sexual activities that are not inside your will and done your way.

In Jesus' Name, Amen.

DAY 26

1 Peter 2:9 NIV "But you are a chosen people, a royal priesthood, a holy nation. God's special possession, that you may declare the praises of him who called you out of darkness into his wonderful light."

This one is for the ladies (sorry fellas) ...

A real woman is a queen, not because she stands strong, but because she fears the Lord! She is never crushed by other people's opinion, because she knows that they are entitled to it. When she finds that her dreams are not being supported, she presses on! "It's ok," she reminds herself, because she's learned that sometimes you may be the only one with a vision. She doesn't have to brag because the fruit of her life is obvious and pure. Envy and bitterness could never consume her because she has learned to prize God's grace. She is often imitated but never duplicated, and if she commends herself, embrace it as your opportunity to take pride in her. Now, let that marinate, and cook it on the grill! lol

If you consider yourself a queen, then you already know the benefits of being you! A lot of people are among us boasting about how they are this and that, and how good of a catch they are, but they can't even tell anybody why. Apart from knowing thy worth, know the benefits of thy worth. It is majorly important! Just like in the game of Checkers, you do all the work to get to the other side. Then, your counterpart has no choice but to crown you once you get there. In life, you have to remember the hard work that God helped you to do. Again, you have to know what you bring to the table so that you will feel comfortable sitting there. Life's trials and tribulations can sometimes make us believe that the sum of our worth is the product of our shortcomings and victories. That's simply untrue. That would mean there are only winners and losers. The fact is that Christ died for us all. We all have the opportunity to be the queens we were created to be. So, don't be fooled!

By the way ladies, saying "He treated me like a queen" when discussing a man who in all truthfulness may have doggy-dogged you does not change the fact that by allowing such treatment, not even YOU were treating yourself like a queen. Pah-lease stop it! Stop confusing the façade of queen treatment with the real thing. A true queen sits with the fact that she was treated beneath her standard and responds accordingly. So, if someone "dogs" her, she handles it properly and not a jewel from her crown is left out of place. We have to learn resilience. It's not just for men. Trust me, I am the most private person you will ever read. However, I still believe in transparency. What I learned from my experiences can help someone else. It brings me tremendous joy to share how the Jesus I serve can carry you through this human journey.

It would be selfish of me to try keeping the fact that God really gave me beauty for ashes a secret. Everyone has an audience. We are all, at some stage in our lives fostering the chance for future queens to learn from our experiences. That's what real queens do. If you are hiding your truth, how can you call yourself a queen? How can you live like you are invisible and expect that you will receive queen-treatment? Being inconsistent devalues you. It is like a person who is known to never keep a friend, dropping names- purely annoying and a complete turn-off. It's a sad day under the sun the way some of us are watering down the quality of QUEENS; which are Omnipotent figures. All queens don't have to be created equal. Just be careful with your associations. That is all.

Dear God,

You care for all humanity. You even care for the animals. As one chosen by you, I pray that I don't let you down.

Please give me the confidence and credence to carry myself in a holy manner; not as a timid weakling afraid of reproach, but as your prized possession commanding recognition of the gift inside of me. I humble myself, and by doing so, you are magnified in me. Since you are the King of Kings; therefore, as long as you live in me, I am royalty. Thank you for giving me a heart for your people and your purposes. Please don't allow me to be crippled with insecurity. Don't let me give away what is precious to anyone or for any reason you don't approve of. I declare that I command the respect, appreciation, admiration, and purposeful interaction that you made me eligible for when you created me.

In Jesus' Name, Amen.

DAY 27

Matthew 7:6 NIV "Do not give dogs what is sacred; do not throw your pearls to pigs. If you do, they may trample them under their feet, and turn and tear you to pieces."

DON'T BE AFRAID TO CASH OUT

A short narrative for depiction purposes: "They wanted something for nothing. So, exclusive to them, she had nothing to give."

That's a story in and of itself, right? Sometimes people try to get over. Let them! Let them get over themselves, over their cold, over the hump, but *not* over on you. I'm not saying pop off at the mouth and troll them. What I'm saying is that there will be times when you will be side-swiped. This doesn't mean retaliate, it means you've identified your teachers. People teach us where they place us on the respect spectrum every time we interact. In these types of situationships, I have learned that responding verbally is not my strength. Instead of engaging in a verbal entanglement, I quietly cash out and leave the table.

We show everyone what our requirements are based on the boundaries we enforce. So, for me, when I remove myself from the equation, I tend to do so without heavily explaining why. If I feel 3% uncomfortable, I'm scooting my chair out from under the table. At 64% uncomfortable, I'm probably not at the table, I'm at the door. Get the picture? And again, not many words are usually involved because I set boundaries from interaction #1. Most of the people who hate me for enforcing boundaries, are the very reasons I have boundaries. The people who mind the most are the reason my boundaries matter. Next time someone turns a blind eye to your value in order that they may abuse an unmerited benefit from you, simply give them the benefit of the doubt - the courtesy of walking away without their head on a stick. *Nothing* for their "troubles." Be still and preserve yourself. Never be intimidated into entertaining what you don't permit. It will never be worth it. If the price of playing the game is your spiritual health, cash out!!!

Heavenly Father,

Thank you for teaching me through your word that I have value. You sacrificed everything, so that I would have access to forgiveness and freedom. When I engage with others, help me to properly assess whether or not continued engagement is spiritually helpful or harmful. You have bestowed some pretty precious blessings upon me, and it is my goal to do with them what you want me to do with them, not that they be squandered or hindered or throttled. Give me the wisdom and courage to know when to set, enforce, and properly uphold the boundaries necessary to foster being a vessel always available for use by you.

In Jesus' Name, Amen.

DAY 28

Romans 12:2 NIV "Do not conform to the pattern of this world, but be transformed by the renewing of your mind. Then you will be able to test and approve what God's will is – his good, pleasing and perfect will."

THE POWER OF DISCERNMENT

A short example of the power of discernment in everyday life would be something like this:

"To her, words weren't a sufficient expression of his intentions. So, she listened. Then, she laughed; giving just enough attention to his actions to derive from them what was needed for her to understand what was on display. After this, she walked away. *Now*, the one listening was him. No longer would his representative suffice and he had to pursue her. That was the only way he would have another opportunity to show her who he actually was. At least that's what he thought. And so, now that he realized the precious gift of her presence, he chased her down; running man style; never to catch her again. You see, he had shown her the first time who he was. The real him, she had already discerned."

I said all that to say this- stop falling for the representative when you can clearly see the entity behind it. Wisdom is borrowed from God. God lends us the discernment to see beyond the surface. His Holy Spirit guides our understanding so that we can see what the operating spirit and motives of a thing are. What most people call intuition, I call the Holy Spirit. An example would be when we know a person is a notorious thief. You enjoy their conversation and they seem like a nice person, but you wouldn't leave them in your home alone. That nudge that told you not to leave them alone with your prized possessions was the Holy Spirit.

The Holy Spirit intercedes for us to God, when we don't know what to say. The Holy Spirit also gives us discernment.

Discernment for me has proven to be the ability to supernaturally distinguish and perceive a danger or eminent reason to fight or flee. It also has served as a sense of perception regarding good and pleasant natured people. In decision making, discernment is a key component. Sound discernment is nurtured only via direct and intimate relationship with God. I will admit that even when I wasn't as close to God as I should have been, God did not take His discernment from me. He is only capable of giving us the real thing – The Holy Spirit. If you notice your discernment is rusty, move a little closer to God. Never settle for those quiet convictions that are easy to ignore. When you notice you are not hearing from the Holy Spirit, remember that God is ALWAYS speaking. It is you who needs to turn up!

Dear God,

Thank you so much for enlightening me with your divine discernment. Thank you for giving me the seal of my salvation in Christ Jesus- your Holy Spirit. Without your Holy Spirit, I would be lost, left to my own devices, and defenseless. Your constant communion with me and meditation in your word fills me with so much of your truth. Spending time with you has really helped me to transform into a good decision maker and has helped me to see clearly. Please don't take your discerning power from me. In fact, I pray that every soul in this world will come to know you and experience your amazing gift of discernment. I pray that you will never allow me to settle for deafened spiritual ears, and that I will always be sensitive to your Holy Spirit. Thank you for empowering me with your revelations, and for all of your generous warnings via sound discernment which keep my head, heart and soul on one accord with your will.

In Jesus' Name, Amen.

DAY 29

Romans 8:18 NIV "I consider that our present sufferings are not worth comparing with the glory that will be revealed in us."

TRAUMA IS NOT THE END

God's omnipotence is truly exemplified through His power to heal us. Healing from emotional trauma, whether of simple or complex nature, is a miracle. Growing up, I never knew that healing wasn't just for sickness. I never knew how God planned to demonstrate his healing through me because I didn't see trauma as something that *could* be healed. I thought, you just walk around with it and like a spider- each time someone or some experience takes a part of you, you just learn to get around without the piece of you that you needed until you grow back what was destroyed. A new set of feelings, forgetfulness, etc.

In my life, I've experienced trauma resulting from the death of loved ones, molestation, divorced parents, rape, sickness, and racism. However, I never realized that *my* trauma was something I could lay down so vehemently. Deliverance from trauma always seemed to be relative to other people. I never felt like my trauma was big or important enough to vocalize. And for some of it, when I *did* attempt to address it, I wasn't met with the supportiveness I needed; no one was really available. But, bless God, one day someone asked me where I saw myself in the next 5 years. I tried, but I couldn't see myself as whole. I saw myself successful but still in pain. That's when I served my trauma its first eviction notice.

All my life, I'd been unnecessarily tainting my life with the pain of my past trauma. Therefore, creating new trauma for myself and sometimes traumatizing others. The truth is that the trauma was crippling me. I had to ask God for help, and what I received was healing. Through mentorship, I learned that God had use for my trauma and that He never intended for it to cripple me. It has taken years of therapy, boundary setting, and determination, to shed the baggage. The biggest blessing in it for me is that I was able to forgive those who traumatized me. I was also able to forgive myself.

When you are on your journey of healing from trauma, don't let anyone shame you for being willing to forgive your oppressors. Through the process, remember that none of us are perfect, but God has accepted us in our imperfect state so that he can perfect us. No, you are not God, but the goal is to be like Him. I'm not saying that forgiveness means that you keep allowing yourself to be abused, but trauma is not the end. It is a marathon, but forgiveness is one of the milestones we all have to reach in order to heal and yield our trauma useful to God.

With that being said, when it comes to emotional trauma, I don't care what you do; If you don't heal, you cannot grow. You will simply be holding yourself hostage. The pain of the traumatic experience will permeate every good place left inside of you unless you do your hard work to come to a place of acceptance and forgiveness. Healing is a by-product of forgiveness. As long as you harbor unforgiveness, the wound left behind from the hurt will not scab over. Instead, it will stay raw. Our society is so far from normalizing *not* being okay. If you don't decide to normalize your own trauma, you will victimize yourself.

Hurt people really do hurt people. The reality is that some of us become so complacent with our trauma that we subconsciously are drawn to more traumatic and chaotic environments and people. Alternatively, a person who has done the hard work of healing from trauma develops such low tolerance for it. For example, I put in so much work to overcome the trauma in my life that I don't care who shames me for getting in the prayer line at church, or for going to talk therapy.

Another thing the healing process developed in me was the ability to apologize more freely. Long story short: I'm always going to do whatever I have to do to be at peace. One of the greatest healing mechanisms is prayer and faster. When we pause, pray, and deny ourselves (fast), we attract God's attention to our situation. God *is* calling you to heal. The trauma was never meant to become your identity.

Refuse to throw your birthright and access to joy aside. Listen, spiders can lose a whole leg and will not stand there angry long enough for you to swat accurately a second time. They have too much life to live lol. The minute you swat at it, it's on the run! And guess what, if you don't kill them, they will heeble-hobble around long enough to regrow the limb you broke off. What an amazing example of the audacity to heal! All from a spider!!! That's how we should be! Sure, you've been hit, but it didn't kill you. Yes, your pain is deep, but it's not too deep for God. Don't let your trauma define you. Forgive the hurt and allow the process of healing to really take hold. Refuse bitterness and stop keeping score. God has a new life for you, and it begins where reliving your trauma ends.

Lord,

Thank you for your healing powers. Even when we do things that we could have otherwise avoided, you are kind enough to reach down and touch us. Your healing makes us whole because you don't half-step anything. Father, I pray for the maturity to be humble. My goal is not to humiliate others by holding back love that you freely have given to me. Help me to treat others how I want to be treated. Help me to yield to your will. I believe you can use my trauma, and I don't want to block your hand. I pray that everyone struggling with any type of trauma will be healed from it and be made whole. Surround me with the support I need to be a victor and give me intolerance for being a victim. Help me not to hurt others. Protect me from hurtful situations. I divorce the pain of my past trauma and embrace your purpose.

In Jesus' Name I pray, Amen.

DAY 30

Psalm 34:17-20 NIV "17 When the righteous cry for help, the Lord hears and delivers them out of all their troubles. 18 The Lord is near to the brokenhearted and saves the crushed in spirit. 19 Many are the afflictions of righteous, but the Lord delivers him out of them all. 20 He keeps all his bones; not one of them is broken."

REJECTION IS NECESSARY

Rejection, rejection, rejection. Accept it. It's a fact of life that not everyone is going to choose you. Swallow that pill; they aren't supposed to. Besides, the healthiest in the yard, is the grass that's shaded. Rain or shine. Even Christ was rejected. John 1:11 NIV "He came to that which was his own, but his own did not receive him." How would you learn the value of acceptance, if you never knew the pain of rejection? Sometimes its warranted, sometimes it's not, but it is always a teacher. It may be painful and feel hurtful initially, but just remember that what you do with rejection is up to you.

Even if it breaks your heart, remember that the aftermath of a breakdown is a breakthrough. Be confident and hold on to your courage. You will always come out on top! A gem cannot be polished without friction; nor a person without trials. The important thing to remember is that rejection is fuel. It can propel you into your next level. However, if you allow it to make you bitter, it will depress your ambition altogether. Either way, always remember that God's love and acceptance of you supersedes any rejection this world can ever inflict.

Lord,

When I encounter rejection, help me to avoid bitterness. In every scenario that doesn't welcome me, help me to gracefully adjust my expectations and find the bright side. I know that rejection is unavoidable in this Christian life, because even Christ was rejected. However, he didn't allow rejection to throw him off course. I ask you for that power- the power to use rejection as fuel and not receive it as fire.

I will not let rejection leave me in a singed state. Since I belong to you, I trust that the pain of rejection will not be permanent. I can do all things through Christ Jesus. Therefore, rejection will not stop me from being all you created me to be. Even when I am not accepted by all, I find renewed joy knowing that I have been accepted by You. I will not live in fear of disapproval. I will not be crushed when the answer is "no." I trust you to fortify my spirit, and to always guard my heart and block rejection from throwing me off of the path that you have carved out for me.

In Jesus' Name, Amen.

DAY 31

Psalm 118:8 NIV "It is better to trust in the LORD than to put confidence in man."

YOU *CAN'T* KEEP YOURSELF

Keep yourself prayed up. Keep yourself accountable. Keep your nose clean. All that is fine, but we must never forget that God is the employer and we are the employee. God is the boss, and I personally take joy in my role as the subordinate because I tend to yield some pretty heavy duty lifting to God. You and I only have one set of eyes. Whether pretty brown, or garden green, none of our eyes enable us to watch our own backs. That's why you have got to be exclusive about entrusting things to God. Truly we have no business entrusting our wellbeing to anyone else. We also have no right to fault others when they failed at looking out for us, because are GOD's responsibility.

We are a God job. It is His mercy, His provisions, His protection, and His forgiveness that we receive and thrive off of. You cannot be self-sufficient in Gods Kingdom. If you are in the Body of Christ, you have the fringe benefit of being fully dependent on Him. You can have a level of established trust between you and another person, but on both ends of that spectrum are imperfect human beings. I, you, them, none of us are our brother or sister's keeper. No matter how much some like to hear themselves say it. Only God is the only constant Keeper. Keep the faith, and with the Lord- make sure you keep in touch.

Dear God,

You are truly my keeper. I am so grateful for your constant favor and provision. You have blocked my demise when I didn't even see it coming. You have healed me from what I didn't know could have made me sick. Thank you for your miracles when I didn't know how I would make it. Thank you for your way of escape from situations that crushed me to the point I didn't feel like I could breath.

When everything around me was out of control, you gave my spirit peace. When my back was against the wall, you took my place. When I had no one to turn to, you reminded me that you were there all along. As I live each day in your care, I ask you to continue to keep me like only you can. Keep me in a way that will let others know I am your child, and draw them nearer to you. Let my soul always rejoice in you and let my life always be in the palm of your hand. Please Lord, always keep me.

In Jesus Name, Amen.

DAY 32

James 1:2-4 NIV "2 Consider it pure joy, my brothers and sisters, whenever you face trials of many kinds, 3 because you know that the testing of your faith produces perseverance. 4 Let perseverance finish its work so that you may be mature and complete, not lacking anything."

PASS THE TEST

Challenges will develop you if you don't allow them to discourage you. There is something unique and special in all of us that the "good times" simply do not bring out. Some of us never knew we could sing until we had to sing to uplift a loved one's spirit. You may not have felt you were good at parenting, but then you mentored a fatherless or motherless child. Since sorrow didn't overtake you, it let you know how strong you really are. Grief is still not easy, but at least it taught you that God could heal.

Not every snare set before you is meant to harm you. Many times, we blame the devil for our troubles. However, it might bless your soul to consider that even the devil can only do to you what God will allow. Now, just because your trial was rough, and God allowed it, doesn't mean He is a careless God. That's not the case at all. God knows our strengths and our weaknesses because he created us. He knows what's inside of us because most of what's inside of us, *He* put it there. Sometimes he allowed you to stumble so that you could begin to give order to your steps. Maybe you needed to learn patience and He allowed some of what you've been through help you regain a healthy pace.

Your scars will be evidence that you took a fall, but the bible tells us in Proverbs 24:16 NIV "for though the righteous fall seven times, they rise again,". Allow God to take the lead in your life. See the pressing as the teacher and yourself as the pupil. Yes, it may feel like its lasting too long, and it may be difficult, but we are the best of students when we learn to eat the meat and throw away the bones. Pass the test so you won't have to take it again.

Lord,

Thank you for being my God. In every trial, I will rejoice because I know that you will give me the victory. I know that you will not allow what I cannot handle. Therefore, in the midst of every pressing and in the mosh pit of every crushing in my life, I trust you to rescue me. I am not cursed with a curse, so I know I will still see your goodness in this land of the living. No pressure will blow me away. No fire will keep me from what you have for me. I will emerge with my spirit restored and my faith strengthened. In all things, good or bad, I will trust you. No test will leave me defeated. I shall have the victory.

In Jesus Name, Amen.

DAY 33

Ephesians 4:32 NIV "Be kind and compassionate to one another, forgiving each other, just as in Christ God forgave you."

FORGIVENESS IS FORGETTING

Pursue a forgetful love, and hopefully that same love will find you. Forgive and be penetrated by the light of Christ, or remain in unforgiveness and be sucked into the darkest place imaginable. The choice is yours.

Start by surrendering your agenda for the person that hurt you. It's the only way you will be able to fully appreciate the matchless abilities of God in an unforgiving situation. I'm not saying you won't experience Him in the mightiest capacity if you don't surrender, I'm just pretty sure its pleasing to Him when we submit. *Especially* since He knows what is best for you. The fact is, someone may hurt you and transition into eternity before they say they are sorry for *how* the hurt you. Imagine that. The moral of this story is: forgive as fast as you can. Turn the battle over to GOD. Forgive and forget. Free up your mind space. Think about how forgiving The Lord has been towards you. It's the only way to reclaim your time.

Dear God,

Thank you for your forgiveness and for your forgetfulness towards our sin. I'm not perfect, but you let me start out with a clean slate over and over again. This doesn't mean I am permitted to go on repeating the same mistakes. Your forgiveness empowers me to be the change I want to see. I need your love and I want to spread the same love and forgiveness towards others that I so generously have received.

While I have your attention, I forgive others for what they have done that hurt me. For the things that I've done which made me feel like I let myself down, I forgive myself. Please forgive me for my sins against you; those of commission and omission. Help me to avoid bitterness, backbiting, slander, and hatred towards others. I know that by forgiving quickly, I am free to receive forgiveness from you for my shortcomings. Therefore, I humble myself and pray that you will keep my heart towards others pure, and my own conscious clean.

In Jesus Name, Amen.

DAY 34

Romans 3:23 NIV "For all have sinned and fall short of the glory of God,"

PERFECT WHERE?

Leave room for error. None of us can afford to point the finger. Yep, I said none of us. The way I see it, metaphorically, we all live in a glass house without tints. This is what has helped me to be free of what other people think and say, and I believe this philosophy will free you too! Life is not about perfection. Of course, it is important to remember God's standard, but it's an unhealthy and unbecoming life habit to be *overly* self-critical. All work and no play? Not recommended! Life with God is an *abundant* life. Being too busy to enjoy the life God has provided for you is unattractive to others who may not know him. Remember, someone is always watching. Even people who dislike you are still paying attention.

I've seen plenty of folk walking around with the world on their shoulders. And for what? Like, who made you God? My dear, the answer is NOBODY!! The first thing said when you get overwhelmed will be: "Even the strong people need to be weak sometimes". Oh, ya think? See no one told us we had to be strong to begin with. Strength is *encouraged,* but no one has the ability to be perfectly strong all the time. If you keep trying so hard to be perfect, you will look like what you've been through at some point. Please, accept that you are an imperfect human being who at best, needs a perfect God. Stop inundating your spirit. We have repentance available to us for a reason. Be human and let God do the heavy lifting.

God,

You are a perfect God. You are the only God. I don't have a horse in the race if I'm competing with you. Right now, I surrender my need to do everything perfectly and ask that you perfect your purpose concerning me.

I need your help and I am not afraid to admit that I have weaknesses. Thank you for being patient with me and giving me room to grow into who I am called to be. I don't have to be perfect and I apologize for trying to portray that I am. I humble myself and ask you to come into my heart. I need you and I am ready to live for you. I am ready to live and enjoy a blessed life, but I cannot do so in my own strength. Thank you in advance for your acceptance and your help.

In Jesus Name, Amen.

DAY 35

Psalms 33:11 NIV "But the plans of the Lord stand firm forever, the purposes of his heart through all generations."

PURPOSE IS FOR REAL, NOT FOR PLAY-PLAY

In order to be on a level of your own, you must first disown the level that'll never be a true fit: the level of others. Its ok to be inspired, but don't be a copycat. Simply saying "Whatever will be, will be" leaves the hope of your future up to fate. As much as it may seem faith filled, that metaphor is empty of faith. It is an insult to the truth introduced in James 2:26 NIV "so faith without deeds is dead". Therefore, we have to be careful adopting worldly perspectives about our destiny. Instead of leaving your faith up to fate, practice speaking things into existence. You have a purpose to fulfil. If some of us addressed our purpose as much as we acknowledge our pain, we'd be healed by now. Yes, you are a vessel, but you were born full of gifts. Know your place and hold it down. God will take over and distribute what you need and what's best for you from there. Never substitute optimism for your faith.

Dear God,

You have thoughts towards me. Your plans for me may not always be obvious, but I believe that they are always at work in me. Thank you for ordering my steps so that I go where I am supposed to be. Thank you for being at work in me in order that I may positively impact others. Please let me use what you've given me and leave no stone unturned. For your glory, I will live with purpose, on purpose.

In Jesus Name, Amen.

DAY 36

Luke 6:31-36 NIV "31 Do to others as you would have them to do to you. 32 If you love those who love you, what credit is that to you? Even sinners love those who love them. 33 And if you do good to those who are good to you, what credit is that to you? Even sinners do that. 34 And if you lend to those from whom you expect repayment, what credit is that to you? Even sinners lend to sinners, expecting to be repaid in full. 35 But love your enemies, do good to them, and lend to them without expecting to get anything back. Then your reward will be great, and you will be children of the Most High, because he is kind to the ungrateful and wicked. 36 Be merciful, just as your Father is merciful."

LOVE MORE. SAY LESS.

Love is a command. Everyone who does not fulfill Gods command to love, cheats themselves and others. God made each one of us with others in mind. Still lost with where to begin with love? Start with those who have hurt you the most. Perhaps even your enemies. Instead of chatting about your opposition, try loving the hell out of them. Trust me, this goes both ways, because although we don't like to hear it, we are often on the receiving end of this practical act of love. Learn to value your own good qualities and you will have more than enough room in your heart to appreciate the good qualities in others. Someone is always watching. Whether you are the one watching or you yourself are being studied, count it a blessing. Imitation is the greatest form of flattery. Know your strength and maintain your influence. We talk enough about people we don't endorse. Love more. Secure your access to the beauty of what God's command to love provides.

Lord,

Thank you for being the greatest example of love. Help me to love your way. Your word is clear, I should be going above and beyond. That's what I pray you will always help me to do. Lead me and let your altitude supersede my emotions. Just as Christ led by example, so shall I. From now on, I declare that I will love even when the norm is to hate. I will be generous with kindness even when it is not returned. My enemies will experience the You in me. Your mercy towards me has been immeasurable. I pray for the discipline to demonstrate that same lovingkindness to others every day.

In Jesus Name, Amen.

DAY 37

Philippians 2:2 NIV "Then make my joy complete by being like-minded, having the same love, being one in spirit and of one mind."

IT IS YOUR JOB TO FIND YOUR PEOPLE

Pay attention to how people treat you. Words spoken with illegitimate intent will be revealed in time. Truth hasn't met anyone it couldn't set free. It is wise to be mindful of the environments that receive you well and the ones that don't. Appreciation vs. Tolerance, remember? Remember that old saying "know your crowd"? I totally agree with it. This is because, sometimes we force our way into a situation because we *want* to belong. Undoubtedly, trying to be part of the harmonious groove in a circle of friends is normal, but if you aren't received well, it is your job to gracefully exit the circle *with love.*

It is possible to mess up the harmony by trying to correct the tune. Sometimes a person or group of people ARE simply out of your league. You have the right to exit patterns of association that don't fit you. It may only be for a season, or it *may* be for life. Either way, you don't have to be the elephant in the room. You *can* leave. And don't go killing nobody with kindness if you aren't really, in your heart, being kind. That's not what powerful, God serving people do.

When you invest time where you belong, you nurture your purpose. When you invest time where you don't belong, you snuff out the fire that fuels your creativity and influence. Why do that? Trust God to plant you in the village you need and were created to be part of. Get in where you actually fit in. When you realize that you march to the beat of a different drum than the next person, that's okay. It doesn't necessarily make them or you bad, real, or fake. It may mean that God has use for you in a different band.

Accept your new norm. As long as you can see that you are positioned in place where God wants you to be, all is well.

Lord,

Thank you for planting me where I can be of best use to you. Harmony is created within me when I am where you want me to be. Concerning my circle of friends, help me to identify where I belong. I don't want to be out of order. Help me to invest time in the right causes. Help me to find my way and my people. No one has to be the bad guy, I just want to be in the right place at the right time, every time.

In Jesus Name, Amen.

DAY 38

Hebrews 11:1 NIV "Now faith confidence in what we hope for and assurance about what we do not see."

NOW FAITH

Faith has no ceiling. Strong faith is the only faith! Not even Jesus was a punk. He was the meekest of all & he still found the will to die for our sin. Step up to the plate and live your life because faith without works *is* dead. Do what God has empowered you to do. Do it even if you have to do it scared. Stop treating God like a discount- only trusting him for a portion of what he has for you!!! You have to believe God for everything! EVERYTHING!!! He will never fail! His Grace gives us confirmation that it's all good. His Mercy gives assurance that it's all GOD. Each day going forward is a blessed one when we learn to Let Go and Let God! It's as easy as you make it, and its $free.99. Besides, the longer you carry your own burdens, the heavier they get.

Dear God,

I approach your throne with my heart open asking you to increase in me. Let your presence affirm my faith always. I pray that I will forever believe in you wholeheartedly. Thank you for always listening when I pray. Even when I don't know what to say, I will give you praise because you already know my heart. Please cover me and guard my heart so that the enemy won't overturn the seeds of faith and encouragement that are sewn in my spirit. Give me the Mind of Christ, so that I will always know that serving you is a reason to live. Help me to inspire others to walk in faith. You have never failed and you won't start now. Even when the way is cloudy, your will is still at work. Faith in you is my light in a dark season. Thank you for your faithfulness.

In Jesus' Name, Amen.

DAY 39

1 Kings 5:4 NIV "But now the Lord my God has given me rest on every side, and there is no adversary or disaster."

"BUT GOD" MOMENTS MATTER

When I see that "But God" in scripture, I know there is about to be a shift. "But God" signifies a move of God. It's such a blessed assurance to be able to reflect on moments in life when I clearly seen God move and meet my needs. When I thought there was no way out of a situation, God got in it. When I was too weary but knew I had to go through, God carried me. In prayer, I get a hunch from the Holy Spirit; a reminder of where God has brought me from. Sometimes I'm riding down the road and a flash back of something I survived comes over me. So, if you see me pulled over on the side of the road dancing and or clucking like a chicken, that's just me praising God for putting His "but" in my situation. I've even given God praise in a fast food drive-thru. He is truly an anyplace, anytime God!

Because of the many "But God" moments in my life, I have developed a posture of gratitude that is evident even when I am in the midst of a difficult and trying time. I know my imperfections are there, yet, God has delivered me from the bondage of harping on them. I can feel a shift and begin resting my mind rather than self-loathing, because I know my deficiencies are covered by the blood of Jesus. I don't believe any of us really have any idea how many "But God" moments we have truly had. However, the ones we are able to perceive are enough for us to praise God forever, because that is truly how long He is worthy. The way my blessings have been set up, I'm of the belief that God is constantly putting His "But" in the way of my demise. It's about trust! Want relief? Surrender your thoughts. There is a "But God" moment is assigned to all of your problems.

Dear God,

Thank you for putting your "but" in my situations. A move from you has been my saving grace on many occasions, and I welcome your divine action. Please continue to shift whatever is necessary for your purpose to be achieved in me and around me. I love to see it. If not for your intercession, I don't know where I would be. You are welcome to "But God" moment me anytime. In fact, I turn everything over to you. Handle me as you will. I trust you and I'm depending on you.

In Jesus Name, Amen.

DAY 40

John: 14:27 NIV "Peace I leave with you; my peace I give you. I do not give to you as the world gives. Do not let your hearts be troubled and do not be afraid."

PROTECT YOUR PEACE

I made a commitment to be a good steward of the peace God grants me by declaring the following: My peace is too valuable to be concerned with who approves of my happiness. The magnitude of favor and blessings I've received are too precious to jeopardize with illegitimate company and purposeless activities. I care less about who leaves, and devote my focus on sharing good vibes with those whose presence brings positive impact. In every season of my life, I'm about planting seeds where there is good soil. My time is not just free space, I'm particular about who occupies my moments. Gone are the days when I entertained nurturing what refuses to grow. People whose life lantern is dark do not have the authority to rob me of the oil that keeps mines shining. No longer do I welcome the glow leaches.

The best thing you can do when you encounter peace killers is Free yourself. If God releases me to severe ties, I cut the strings. Stop letting people speak things into your life that God never intended to be there. Know what you know and be careful. You, nor I, want to get spoiled on wrong beliefs. Surrounding yourself with like-minded believers is a key first step. However, adopting healthy expectations and boundaries are equally as important. You can't get to the right place with the wrong people. Setting boundaries for others without establishing boundaries for yourself is a lost cause.

Yes, we definitely have to stand firm in what we expect from others so that we don't emit a confusing and irrational nature. What are the boundaries you've set for yourself? Do you sit through every conversation to demonstrate respect for others? Or, are there some topics you simply won't tolerate yourself discussing? What do you eat and how much? Or, will you eat anything to satisfy your human hunger out of convenience? Are you interested in specific things, or is anything game?

WE have to know what WE are about before we can define the qualifications for people in our lives. For example, I am highly opposed to unchaperoned sleepovers. If my children go to a sleepover, *I'm* going to a sleepover. Meaning, I'm going to be at the one they are attending. Period lol. Not that I sit in a seat of judgement towards parents who parent differently, but my boundaries are my boundaries.

I tend gravitate towards people who share the same core values as me, and I tend to attract people who respect boundaries as well as set them. When it comes to preserving peace, I believe it is important to steer clear of things that mirror a chaotic mindset. Clutter, for example. When I notice clutter in my home or vehicles, I know that chaos has snuck into my spirit somewhere. My peace barometer also registers differently depending on my interactions with others. If I find myself engaging in conversations that facilitate me reliving chaotic experiences, the first thing I do is take a break from leisure talk for a bit. This helps me throttle codependency on toxic relationships and associations.
Part of protecting the peace God has bestowed on us to remember what God has already done. However, you don't have to live in the past to give God glory for what he has already done for you. Your testimony isn't just for others, it is also for you.

Your past peace has a purpose, and while you should always leave room for the new level of peace in your heart, never forget your humble beginnings. Protecting your peace is a reasonable service. Alternatively, glorifying past shortcomings is unreasonably draining. So, cut off the glow leaches, remember your best moments, and expect God to pour out more peace than you have room to receive. Be a beacon of God's marvelous light.

Father God,

As I travel this life's journey, I ask that your peace which surpasses all comprehension will continuously be in me. You are a generous God, and I believe that you can give me every ounce of calm and pause that I need. In moments of chaos and haywire, please let your peace abide in me. Block every peace leach; seen and unseen. Let me be good ground, and sew your seeds of peace in me. I want to be a lighthouse, but I need your precious oils of truth and love to do so. I declare that no one shall rob me of the peace that you have given me. My home is peaceful. I have peace on my job. My marriage is peaceful. In my family, we have peace and harmony. I accept your peace and glorify you now for lending it to me.

In Jesus Name, Amen.

BONUS DAYS

DAY 41

1 Timothy 5:8 NIV "Anyone who does not provide for their relatives, and especially for their own household, has denied the faith and is worse than an unbeliever."

ALL IS WELL

Where are the wells? In biblical days, wells were part of the legacy left behind to future generations. Wells symbolized life, prosperity, and longevity because of the precious resource they encase – water. They established a family's birthright to remain in a certain place. It's interesting how historic civilizations seemed to have done *more* with *less*. As parents and surrogate parents, we should value the power and impact of leaving a legacy. Without prioritizing the importance leaving a strong legacy, we perpetuate undue hinderance on our children and future generations- a self-manufactured crisis.

What's upsetting is the fact that some people spend parenthood capitalizing off of their children's existence, all while never actually investing into their children future. Instead of leaving a well, some parents leave dams; holding back floodwaters of obligations rather than benefits. When we receive children from God, they are teachers. It is not our responsibility to project an identity onto them. Instead, we are charged with leading them to God as they are.

Too many of us spend years diminishing a child's core identity, so that they will fit into the ideals we have for them. Your son is 6ft, so he can't be a scientist - he has to be a basketball player. You are determined that your daughter is going to be a lawyer, even though she is divinely gifted at singing and songwriting. Sound familiar? One thing I learned as a child was that parenting is not supposed to be about abusing your role. Now, as a mother, I am careful to utilize my influence to lead my children in the right direction, rather than forcefully projecting my identity onto them, simply because I can.

I am leading a life before them that demonstrates my dependence on God's omnipotence and His ability to provide. Yes, they receive discipline and constructive correction, but emotional parenting is not my practice. We surround them with love and truth, but just like the Bible does not demonstrate emotional parenting, seldom do we. Having children and failing to devote time towards leaving a legacy is like seasoning meat only to rinse the seasoning off before it hits the grease- it's pointless.

God gives each of purpose before we get here. So, with our children, we have the privilege of enhancing what is already there. As long as they are in your care, it is your responsibility to provide your children with what they need to become a productive member of society, so don't wait until the last minute to do what is necessary to give them a good start. A failure to plan on your part will constitute an emergency on theirs. How unfair is that?

Wealth is not just about money. As a parent, our affirmation, love, and encouragement towards our children are among the thing's money can't buy. Humility is also a vital component of our legacy. Never be above serving your children or too good to provide supportive affirmations like "it's ok, I've failed before too," or "don't worry about it, I got you," or "I'm still grateful for you." Do all you can to ensure that your precious babies don't grow up seeking seasoning from all the wrong places because they didn't get it at home. Mothers- love your daughters- don't compete with them. Fathers- encourage your sons and proactively teach them so that they can avoid having to learn the hard way. Impart the discipline of properly managing finances and resources into your children so that they won't squander their increase on things that don't increase their value.

Successful people learn the importance of investing in themselves early on. As a godly parent, its only right that you also educate your kids about the biblical principle of tithing. God owns everything and a solid understanding of where all blessings truly flow from will serve them well in life. Just like marriage, three people should be in the parentship- you, your child, and God. Church doesn't have to be the first place they learn about God. They should see evidence of God in you. Exposing them to the gospel of Jesus once they reach an age of understanding will help develop their appetite for spiritual edification.

I know this is a lot, but it's necessary, and it's feasible if you take your time. Just remember the patient and generous legacy of God. Always keep in mind the grace of God towards you. You'll need it for those moments when taking your break-up, lay-off, or disappointment out on your child seems unavoidable. No matter how ratchet you are, God keeps blessing you, rewarding you, taking care of you, and forgiving you. He is laying up riches for who? YOU! Remember that when you are raising children. The legacy you leave is up to you.

Lord,

Thank you for your illuminating word. Thank you for always having us in mind. Throughout your word, you have given us so many examples of leadership, love, and relentless provision; all of which are exemplary of your lordship and legacy. Please continue to empower us to share wisdom and wealth, and to lead a life that leaves a legacy that points future generations to you. I humble myself because it is not about me. Everything you do through me is for your glory.

As a leader and pioneer in my family, I ask that you download unto me every principle and discipline that I need to properly sew into the lives of those you grant me access to. Thank you for those that you have placed in my path to steer me in your direction. Increase in us and let your presence within us manifest outside of us. I declare generational blessings forever over my family and the entire body of Christ. We are your chosen people. We are the head and not the tail. We will operate as such.

In Jesus' Name, Amen.

DAY 42

Psalms 133:1 NIV "How good and pleasant it is when God's people live together in unity!"

So, you're family. You know? That good old "blood is thicker than water," "that's my bloodline," "family over everything," right? Well, what if you are dealing with a jealous parent or sibling? What about the black sheep of the family? Proverbs 11:29 explains how we gain nothing when we bring trouble to our family. But what if we are born into a family where dysfunction is already there? What if there is abuse in our family? What about when we are accosted by negative spirits in our family? Well, God has an answer! You Love!

No, it will not be easy to crawl over, under, or through the dysfunction, but love pardons the dysfunction long enough for you to come out of a crooked situation, straight. And, if you can find the strength to cast off the spirit of oppression that most surely will be the product of any fake love from bloodline relatives, you may actually learn something. Don't get it twisted, not everybody in your bloodline is truly your family!!! Truth be told, y'all may share a blood relation, but nothing else.

Of course, we are all here for a divine reason, but does that mean we accept those who haven't accepted us in order to figure it out? Not at all. You see them at the "family" cookout, but do you trust them with your kids? To support your business ventures without receiving a handout? To call you sometime? Be honest and accept it if the answer to that question is no! Sometimes we continue to fellowship with bloodline relatives when it is clear that the relationship is fruitless and toxic.

You have your Ruth's and you have your Orpah's. The Ruth's are the ones that are loyal, honest, and who share the same core values as you. You and your Ruth's may not see eye to eye all the time, but most of the time, the relationship is harmonious and peaceful. You uplift one another and God is truly at the center of your relationship. On the opposite side of the spectrum, are the Orpah's. Orpah is the bloodline relative that you love, but at some point, the toxicity of the relationship forces you to love them from a distance. Examples of Orpah's are: You and them can gossip together but nothing more; If you need money, they wouldn't loan you a nickel, even if they owed it to you; You invite them but they never support your events; Or, they come to all of your events, but only to speculate, never to genuinely celebrate. These are what we call bloodline relatives. It is true that we are still commanded to love them, but they are not family.

Over the years, I believe that I have finally come to understand what family really is! That's right, I cracked the code (lol). First of all, your family in Christ *is* your family. I mean, the people whose company, behavior, purpose, and presence compliment yours and don't disrupt your status with Christ. Useful relationships. True believers of Christ. The God-sent surrogates who stand in the gaps for you when your biological family members abandon you. Those whose fellowship is edifying and clearly tied into purpose. Your vibe plus theirs is organic and fruitful. Relationships that bridge gaps between hurt and healed. Bonds that opened doors for you when all others were shut (without a fee they did this).

Don't get me wrong, not all access worth having should be given for free, but those interactions that make you feel caffeinated after draining tribulations - they are your motivators. Your true family members are the people who are happy for you and know how to celebrate you no matter what a nay-sayer broadcast. They are your accountability partners. They are the people who make it their business to bless you and whose prayers include you.

Family supports, commits, celebrates, and prunes you with love. They do not say they love you but demonstrate direct hatred, refuse to share in your joy, speak, teach, or condone anything offensive or destructive to your purpose and faith. When you look at the biblical definition of love in 1 Corinthians 13:4-8- you see them. You will know them by their contributions towards not only you, but also others.

Family is a feel-good place, but it's not a platform for fake love. Real family respects you, for you without ceasing, and shows you agape love. You will inevitably be attracted to them. They draw you in and in feels like home! A lot of people have countless relatives, yet they are still in search of true family members. It's majorly necessary that we know the difference, so that we don't omit to divorce ourselves from the erosive relations, or fail to identify the relations which we should commit engage in. The revelation of "who is who" comes from The Lord himself, through time spent before Him regarding who your people are.

So, pray! Ask God to remove those people who are not in your life for the right reasons according to his will for your life, and watch how folk you thought were family dissipate into the fog. Once you see who is left, you will automatically know. No, it won't be comfortable at first, but you will adjust. The sooner you know, the sooner you can grow.

Lord,

Thank you for giving me the capacity to love others despite the circumstances. Please give me the discernment I need to articulate the difference between those whom you have chosen for me to do life with and those whom you've designated as love opportunities along the way. I pray that every iota of strife, jealousy, division, fake love, weakness, selfishness, scornfulness, idolatry, and demonic presence be wiped from my family. It is my prayer that you will restore and sustain unity in my family. We are not in competition with one another, we are in love with one another. Every conflict is resolved and every entanglement is neutralized, in The Name of Jesus. Your intended purpose for family and fellowship abound in my bloodline, and within my family lineage. We shall love one another and support one another. I rebuke every divisive alliance and association that seeks to disguise itself as family, but really seeks to destroy family. I rebuke incest, negligence, biasness, and confusion in my family. Please keep us in good standing with you and help us to be properly impactful on other families who may be watch us.

In Jesus' Name, Amen.

DAY 43

Galatians 1:10 NIV "Am I now trying to win the approval of human beings, or of God? Or am I trying to please people? If I were still trying to please people, I would not be a servant of Christ."

DON'T MAKE COMPARISON YOUR CAUSE

You ever seen someone with a hairstyle, or nail shape, or outfit that looked amazing on them, but when you got that exact thing yourself, it looked terrible? It's an interesting phenomenon isn't it? Over the years, I've discovered that what is right for one person, may not be equally appropriate for the next. What God has for you is for you; that's what I chalk it up to. Likewise, what God has for someone else is for them. When we put trust in the process instead of into God, we forfeit the divine affirmation that keeps us from expecting someone else's results.

Comparison robs us of the joy and appreciation that should be experienced when something good happens for ourselves and others. Practicing acceptance and surrender helps us to release the need to compare or compete. It's important to reach a place of contentment with where we are in our own lives so that we don't miss the inspiration other people's accolades have to offer us. Get your life!! If you are wondering why you're down, bitter, and in a sunken place, it's possibly because you've disallowed yourself to celebrate others.

Don't be that person who secretly is empowered by someone else's greatness, but doesn't show It until you're at their funeral. We see this ALL THE TIME, and it's sad. Why is it that people sometimes die before anyone decides to share in their life's joy? It's sad watching a person get so consumed with competing and comparing themselves to others that they don't learn how to do anything else in life. Some of yall are out here competing with everyone – your daughter, son, sister, friend, your boss; and it's a vicious cycle.

They have a baby - you have a baby. They get promoted - you're in HR filing a grievance. They work from home - here you come with telecommute requests. They get a new car - you get a new truck. They publish a book - now you are writing a book. They buy y'all child a basketball - you buy them a motorbike. You are not inspired, you are competing! It's unhealthy and exhausting and it shows. Do you understand now why your always tired? It's not *your* work you are doing, you're just working.

The first step is to stop perpetuating competitiveness and perpetuate unity. Constantly trying to trump the next persons accolades distracts you from blessing God for your own! God forbid you carry the insecurities into parenthood; you may unknowingly provoke sibling rivalry among your own children. A posture of comparison is toxic. Research shows that toxic people become toxic parents and the evidence of this is sibling rivalry among their children. They play up one child's worth and value at a time so that they can maintain emotional control over the other children who then begin competing for their love.

Eventually, the successor of that sibling rivalry gets the grand prize of competition between themselves and their parent! Is this you? Is this *about* to be you? Let me be the first to tell you that it doesn't have to be. You can cast down the insecurities that make you feel like you have to compete before more damage is done. Declare and decree that what God has for you is for YOU, and divorce the events that propelled you into such self-hate and self-sabotage. If what I'm saying resonates with you- stop trying to walk a mile in other people's shoes. Comparison has consumed you for long enough, it's time to come out!!! So, Come out!!! Remind yourself that the road is straight and narrow and it is wide enough to share.

Dear God,

Today, I call out to you, requesting humbly that you rescue me from the bondage of comparison. Lord, remove the spirit of jealousy, envy, pride, and insecurity from me, and please do not ever let me be entangled in it again. I ask that if there is any secret place in my heart and soul where the root of ungratefulness is holding space, please evict it. What you have for me is for me, and what you have for me is too precious for me to diminish simply because I am distracted. Help me to celebrate, appreciate, and uplift others genuinely; knowing that in due season the harvest you have for me. I am grateful, blessed, adequate, whole, useful. I am who you say I am.

In Jesus' Name, Amen.

ACKNOWLEDGEMENTS

Lord,

I want to thank you for all the work that you have done in me, for all the love that you have poured into me and spread through me, for your grace, and for your tender mercies towards me. I can never repay you, but I pray that you will be glorified in the highest forever. You are my maker, my keeper, and my help. I owe it all to you. Let this journal and everything in it glorify you and serve your perfect purpose in the life of every soul it reaches. Thank you for using me as a mouthpiece to edify your beloved.

In Jesus' Name, Amen

Also,

I would like to express my love and appreciation to my husband Tom, and my children Thomas, Jr., Violet, and Hazel. I love you and everything I do under what I do for God, is for you. To my mother, father, and every single one of my family members; the Spruell's, Tillery's, Crosson's, Graham's, Davis', Primas, Capers, Dinkins', Drakeford's, Perry's, Moore's, Henley's, Bigelow's, Mayfield's, Perkin's, Lane's, Clarke's, Woods, all yall- Thank you for the love and support I have so generously received. I love yall!

To my church family at First Baptist Church of Glenarden, and to my home church family at New Samaritan Baptist Church- I love you and sincerely thank you. To my day 1 friends and rollies: Flo, DeAnna, Shanta, Danni, Alana, Quanny, LaShawn (STINK), Toya, Shatia, Bre, Randi, Chelarr, and Justice- yall are amazing and I am blessed to have soul sisters like you. To my mentors and prayer partners Elder Brenda Woods, Joyce Daniels, Takia, Aunt Shanna, Aunt DeeDee, Aunt Lawanda, and Pat- Thank you all so much for laboring in love with me over the years. I am so grateful for each of you and that God assigned me to such beautiful, passionate, selfless, and godly women.

Lastly, I want to thank my NC A&T SU family (AGGIE PRIDE), Candy Jackson, Robin Lea, LaTosha Lea, Lisa Lea, Mary Studham, Kathleen Brown, Naya Bethea, Shanna Johnson, Reverend Gentry, Pastor Qwame, Diane, Aunt Michelle, Paulette, Donnie, my doctors, and everyone who made themselves available to me for inspiration, education, knowledge, and empowerment through this process. To everyone who this book touches – Thank you and may God keep you and bless you.

God's Peace, Love, Joy & Light,

Sarah

EMERGENCY CONTACTS

Reassurance – John 6:47

Abandonment – Psalms 34:18

Abuse Recovery – Jeremiah 33:6

Suicidal – Matthew 11:28-30

Rejection – Jeremiah 29:11

Insecurity – Philippians 4:12-13

Identity Issues – Psalms 139:13-14

Grief – Matthew 5:4

Depression – Philippians 4:13

Under Attack – Isaiah 54:17

Letting Go – Job 17:9

Hurt – John 15:18

Unforgiveness – Ephesians 4:32

Lonely – Psalms 139:7-10

Distracted – Matthew 6:33

Frustrated – Romans 8:28

Lost – Isaiah 58:11

Discouraged – Romans 8:18

Breakthrough – Philippians 4:19

Afraid – Isaiah 41:13

Anxiety – Philippians 4:6-7

Healing – Jeremiah 17:14

Addiction – Galatians 5:1

Unsafe – Psalms 91

Feeling Judged – Romans 8:1

Peace – Romans 15:13

Troubled – Psalms 34:17-20

Support – Psalms 55:22

Advice – Psalm 1:1

Defeat – Proverbs 3:5-6

Got A Bad Report – Psalm 112:6-7

Unloved – Isaiah 54:10

Fell Short – Romans 3:23

Empty – Psalms 81:10

Guilty – 1 John 1:9

Resentment – Ephesians 4:31-32

Angry – Psalms 37:8

Overwhelmed – Isaiah 40:31

Tithing – Luke 6:38

Jealousy – Galatians 6:4

Made in the USA
Columbia, SC
26 February 2021